Beautiful Badass

How to believe in yourself
against the odds

Beautiful Badass

How to believe in yourself against the odds

CHRYSTA BAIRRE

Published by
Proud Woman Press
19 Old Town Square, Ste. 238
Fort Collins, CO 80524

Copyright © 2020 Chrysta Bairre

All rights reserved. No part of this publication may be reproduced, stored in a retrieval system, or transmitted, in any form or by any means, electronic, mechanical photocopying, recording, or otherwise, without the prior written permission of the publisher, except by reviewers, who may quote brief passages in a review. For permissions, and information relating to special discounts on bulk orders, write to the publisher at the address provided below, or submit a form at beautifulbadass.me.

ISBN: 978-1-7345841-0-3 (Paperback Edition)
ISBN: 978-1-7345841-1-0 (eBook Edition)

Library of Congress Control Number: 2020902019

SELF-HELP / Personal Growth / Self-Esteem
BODY, MIND & SPIRIT / Inspiration & Personal Growth
BIOGRAPHY & AUTOBIOGRAPHY / Women

This book tells the truth, and truth is subjective. It represents the author's present recollections of experiences over time and recreated with consideration of trauma-related memory gaps, and that's not even considering menopausal brain fog! The stories shared in this book are true to the memory of the author's personal experience. Some names and characteristics have been changed, events have been compressed, and dialogue recreated.

The advice and strategies contained in this book may not be suitable for every situation. Take what you like and leave the rest. These tools are shared with the understanding that neither the author nor the publisher are held responsible for your experience, your life, or any results from the advice in this book.

Illustrations by Ellen O'Neill
Developmental Editing and Copyediting by Alli Martin at Selfwinding Editorial
Proofreading by Bonnie McKnight at Lady McKnight Editing
Cover and interior design by Deanna Estes, LotusDesign.biz

Printed in the United States of America

First printing February 2020

Published by:
Proud Woman Press
19 Old Town Square, Ste. 238
Fort Collins, CO 80524

beautifulbadass.me

This book is dedicated to Christy White,
the little girl who believed in herself enough to keep living.

Contents

Introduction 1

Part 1: Hope

Chapter One: Fired at Forty 7

Chapter Two: Get Gratitude 13

Chapter Three: Random Acts of Self-Kindness 21

Chapter Four: Choose Something Better 25

Chapter Five: Believe in Yourself More Than You Believe Others . . . 31

Chapter Six: Self-Care: Beyond the Basics 39

Chapter Seven: Radical Self-Love 45

Chapter Eight: Overcoming Self-Doubt 49

Chapter Nine: The Seed of Self-Worth 53

Chapter Ten: How to Believe in Yourself When Things Aren't Going Well 57

Chapter Eleven: Don't Quit Before the Miracle 63

Part 2: Courage

Chapter Twelve: Divorced and Bankrupt at Twenty-Nine 71

Chapter Thirteen: Disappointing the Right People 79

Chapter Fourteen: Stop Comparing Yourself to Others 85

Chapter Fifteen: How to Say No 91

Chapter Sixteen: Get Fired Up 97

Chapter Seventeen: Be Awesomely Selfish 105

Chapter Eighteen: Be Demanding 109

Chapter Nineteen: High School Hell 113

Chapter Twenty: Progress, Not Perfection 119

Chapter Twenty-One: Building Confidence 123

Chapter Twenty-Two: Is Life Hard or Easy? 127

Part 3: Create

Chapter Twenty-Three: The Shame of Need 135

Chapter Twenty-Four: My Free Car 139

Chapter Twenty-Five: Receiving is Better than Giving 143

Chapter Twenty-Six: Own Your Awesome 149

Chapter Twenty-Seven: Living with Intention 153

Chapter Twenty-Eight: Stand Up, Speak Up 159

Chapter Twenty-Nine: Desires on Fire 163

Chapter Thirty: Self-Trust and Building Intuition 169

Chapter Thirty-One: Rise To The Challenge 175

Chapter Thirty-Two: Progress Is the New Perfect 179

Chapter Thirty-Three: I Ain't Got No Body 183

Chapter Thirty-Four: Find Your Community 191

Chapter Thirty-Five: Too Big for Your Britches 195

Chapter Thirty-Six: Redeemed 199

Chapter Thirty-Seven: Reality Check: Busting The Myth That
Anything is Possible 203

Chapter Thirty-Eight: It's Time to Tune In 207

Acknowledgements 211

Resources 215

Vocabulary of Feeling Words 217

About the Author 219

Index 221

Introduction

While writing this book I read *You Are a Badass at Making Money* by Jen Sincero. I loved and hated *You Are a Badass at Making Money*.

I loved it because I believe most of the ideas presented in the book, and I truly believe that our minds and hearts, when working as one, are powerful manifestors. We, as human beings, are creators. We create our experience. We create our reality. In this way our power to create is limited only by our beliefs.

The part I hated about *You Are a Badass at Making Money* is the part that overlooked circumstances. If you have experienced or are currently experiencing trauma, mental or chronic illness, or some form of discrimination based on your race, nationality, ethnicity, gender, gender identity, sexual orientation, religion, disability, or another socioeconomic barrier, you can't simply positively think your way around those situations. If you are limited by your circumstances, all this Law of Attraction type stuff isn't going to help you much.

For example, true poverty is a very real barrier you can't think your way around. True poverty limits access to resources, which means fewer advantages when trying to improve your situation. Your level of financial privilege affects the availability of support from family members and friends capable of loaning you money, investing in your education, or connecting you to job opportunities. In Jen's book, she talks about borrowing $85,000 from a family friend. That level of privilege is unrealistic for someone who grew up in poverty. Most truly poor people primarily know other people who are also struggling financially. Not everyone knows someone who has $850—let alone $85,000—to loan to a friend.

Individuals who start with privilege have more resources to begin with, even if they are currently living in a garage like Jen was at the time of her loan. This distinction is important because while people like Jen might find themselves facing hardship, they still have access to more resources in hard times than people like me who were underprivileged and living with trauma for many years.

Yes, your attitude matters. Your beliefs matter. The stories you tell yourself about what you're capable of have a significant influence on what you can create. But you'll be most successful putting that manifesting power into action after your situation has improved and after you're personally safe, stable, and whole.

If you're safe and whole now but you haven't always been that way, you might still have some significant shit to work through. And that's okay. If the trauma in my past has taught me anything, it's that I really am a badass. And I'm a badass who still gets tripped up by my past. The lack of resources and opportunities in my youth continues to have a ripple effect in my adult life. I've had to deal with those hurdles and accept that sometimes, despite my best efforts, I'll get tripped up by them.

Introduction

Being limited by a situational barrier is very different from being limited by mindset. This book is written for those of us who aren't just limited by mindset but by very real situational barriers. This book is for women like me who have been limited by their circumstances. Some of us have struggled since we were young. Some of us are divorced, or struggling to raise children or take care of an aging parent. Some may be unemployed or stuck at the same dead-end job with few opportunities for change or advancement. Some may have been raised in relatively nice, normal families, but are now unfulfilled or underpaid. We are the survivors of classism, racism, poverty, sexual assault, violence, mental illness, addiction, or abuse. We're resourceful. We're resilient. We survived against all odds, and now we're ready to thrive.

This book invites you to find a way to grow that works for you. All the ideas I provide are designed for you to consider, try out, and decide where to take them. Don't just use my suggestions, make them your own! Discover and create more tools to build the better life you want, regardless of the life you were given.

> You can be something. So be the best fucking something you can be.

What is a better life? Well, that depends on you. How do you define "better?" Is it fulfillment in your relationships?

Finding purpose in your work? Making a difference in the world? Maybe it's travel, a healthy long-term relationship, higher personal income, or being debt-free. Whatever it is for you, you can have better. You deserve better. You can't be *any*thing, because of the limitations imposed by circumstances, but you can be *some*thing. If you're done living your life for everyone but you, I promise it only gets better from here.

Part 1: Hope

This is a story of hope, courage, and creation. It's my story, but it's really about you. It's about what my story means to you. How my story speaks to you. What my story inspires you to do. Because that's how it really works—we don't inspire ourselves, we inspire each other.

Throughout this book I share parts of my story, and through my story I hope you see parts of yourself. Take what you read and use what you can.

This book tells the story of the darkness I fought and defeated to unleash the beautiful badass that's always been inside me. Somewhere in this book is your story, too. Are you ready to embrace your beautiful badass?

Fired at Forty

I've wanted to be an entrepreneur for as long as I can remember. As a young girl, I came up with many different business ideas. These ideas stemmed from my natural creative and enterprising nature, fueled by a desire to shape a better future for myself.

When I was seven years old, my older sister and I dreamed up a pretend radio station. We recorded hours of programming on our family boombox, complete with a station call sign, music (classics of the late 70s and early 80s), hard-hitting interview segments with characters like Wacky Wanda (inspired by Gilda Radner's *Saturday Night Live* character, Roseanne Roseannadanna), and even commercials about soap. I distinctly remember one commercial had me singing a chorus of "soap soap soap soap" behind my sister's voice-over lauding the benefits of the fictional soap product. Those moments are among the few happy memories from my childhood.

In high school, I developed a concept for a used bookstore and cafe. The shop would have plenty of cozy reading nooks, couches, and space to hold meetings for book clubs and theater groups. I pictured a checkerboard tile floor in warm tones with layered oriental rugs anchoring a seating area. My best friend Emily and I named the store Dog-Eared Pages. I was so invested in the concept I created business plans. I started collecting inventory and stored dozens of boxes of books in my mom's basement. I eventually abandoned the dream of my bookstore because I lacked the resources to get it started.

I had many other ideas for business ventures throughout the years. Despite my limited circumstances, I never gave up hope that I would one day have a business of my own. I continued to build resources, adjusting and re-adjusting my vision of my place in the world.

By my late thirties, my entrepreneurial ideas manifested in a career coaching business. After years of helping friends and family with their career questions and problems, giving them feedback on resumes, and helping friends prep for interviews using my background in human resources, business management, and my personal experience creating a successful career from limited opportunity, I was finally ready to plan a business launch.

When I was thirty-seven, I quit my full-time corporate job with a plan to build my business while continuing to work part-time. I worked several part-time jobs over the next few years, and I've never worked harder. As it turned out, working "part-time" actually meant I produced a similar volume of work to previous full-time jobs, doing so in fewer hours for a lower hourly rate with zero benefits.

Three years after quitting my full-time job, I was working part-time as an accounting manager at a local accounting firm, and as my 40th birthday approached, I knew it was time to take a leap of faith or give up on my dream. (Giving up was not an option I was seriously considering.)

My motivation to make the leap to business owner without the security of part-time employment was only partially related to turning forty. My boss at the accounting firm was one of the top three worst bosses I'd ever encountered. She was a coward, a liar, and a bully. She was also one of the best bosses I'd worked for. She trusted me with projects I was afraid to take on, and every time she trusted me, I rose to the challenge. She pushed me into deeper water and, as it turned out, I found I could swim.

As my confidence rose with every challenge she put in front of me, I found my ability to work for a passive-aggressive boss was wearing thin. I began planning my exit, but she fired me before I could quit.

I found myself suddenly without a crutch job. It was the best gift she could have given me. One last time she forced me into a situation I wasn't sure I was ready for, and once again I faced the challenge. No more excuses. It was time to quit planning and start my business for real.

One week after getting fired, I enrolled in a high-end business coaching program. I knew I wanted the support and resources to build a successful business rather than learn through trial and error as I had previously done out of necessity. I saw my investment in this program equivalent to earning a college degree. I had skipped college because I was too poor and too busy learning to manage anxiety, depression, and PTSD to pursue higher education. But now I wanted to pursue the exact education that I needed to create a successful business.

> Doing what's expected doesn't always get you what you want.

I had no idea how I was going to make the nearly $1,000 monthly payment. It was a major investment, and my typically frugal then-partner surprised me when he agreed we'd make it work. Somehow, month after month, I made the payment for my business program—sometimes by the skin of my teeth. It was one of the scariest decisions I ever made—particularly for a girl who lived in poverty for years. Spending that amount of money was a significant commitment and an act of faith and trust in myself.

My intuition played a part in making this decision, too. I'm not sure I can quite explain how I knew, but somehow I knew investing in my future this time was worth the risk. Playing it safe doesn't always pay off. Doing what's expected doesn't always get you what you want. I thought of all my friends, family, and coworkers who invested tens of thousands of dollars in college degrees. A few found their calling and were happy with their investment. Far more of the people I knew were struggling to pay off student loans well into their late thirties and forties, often not earning much more than I made in my accounting career. What do you do when you have access to the right tools and resources, and you do the work, and you still end up miserable and broke?

I took a big risk and it was worth it—which isn't to say taking a risk is always the right thing to do. In my situation I got sick of my own excuses and wasn't willing to keep doing something that wasn't working. I spent years researching and planning my business and it was time to either fail or succeed.

I can look back on the start of my business and acknowledge making smart choices. I have the luxury of knowing in hindsight that it was worth it. But the day I started my business and the day I invested in coaching, I didn't have the benefit of hindsight. I had plenty of doubt. I had plenty of fear. And I had plenty of faith. I didn't know it would work out but I believed it *could*. As I had many times before in my life, I made something from next-to-nothing.

No matter how stuck you might feel, I believe there are nearly infinite possibilities ahead of you. There's some idea or dream that's been with you for a long time. Maybe it's been with you so long you barely notice it anymore. Maybe you shoved that dream down because life got in the way and you became so busy dealing with the next crisis that your dream is practically a memory. Maybe you spent so many years surviving that you don't know another way. At some point you have to take a leap of your own. Maybe it will work out the way you want, maybe it won't. You won't know if you don't try.

Get Gratitude

One of the most effective and easiest tools to create health, success, and happiness in work and life is gratitude. In the beginning, gratitude gave me hope when I had little else to count on. Gratitude is where I started, so we'll start there, too.

Growing up in poverty and with domestic abuse and mental illness, I became very aware of the danger in my home, and in the process I became attuned to everything that was bad. I learned to read the room, to watch for signs that my alcoholic stepfather was drunk, and to identify when my mom was mentally and emotionally absent, all so I could try to take care of and protect myself from abuse and neglect. Years later, after my mom attempted to take her own life and was admitted to the psychiatric ward multiple times, I watched her carefully for signs of instability or self-injury. I thought, if I could see the danger coming, maybe I could avoid the worst of it. My vigilance backfired—in keeping a weather eye for danger, I created anxiety and depression.

Constantly being on the lookout for what was unsafe at home meant living in a state of fight-or-flight. Living in survival mode means rarely, if ever, letting your guard down. There's no time to relax. You're too busy watching for the next thing that might go wrong. This habit of looking for things to go wrong, of noticing every potential threat, continues even after your situation improves. Years later these learned behaviors may still be negatively impacting your life.

Adopting an attitude of gratitude doesn't mean overlooking the bad stuff, or pretending like it never happened. It means being vigilant about noticing the good stuff, too. Just as being attuned to risk and harm creates anxiety, tuning into the good stuff creates feelings of hope and happiness. I could use more hope and happiness, how about you?

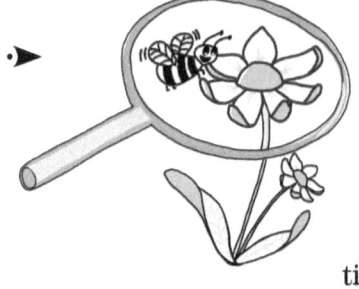

Gratitude is all about (re)training your brain to seek the positive. Most of the time your experience of life is informed by whatever you're paying the most attention to.

In motorcycle safety class, one of the first things you learn is to keep your head up and continually scan the road ahead. If you stare too long at one spot on the road, your mind and body will naturally adjust your course to wherever you're looking. If you're looking at the gutter, you start to drift toward the gutter. Your direction follows your attention.

Want more joy in life? Look for joy. Notice joy. Be open to joy. Be curious about joy. Cultivate joy and you'll experience more joy.

Get Gratitude

• •

Here's an example of how you can start looking for joy in your life:

Instead of a car, I often drove to work on my sapphire blue Honda Metropolitan scooter. My usual route took me over the train tracks running through town. The bumps and dips on either side of the tracks were noticeable when driving in a car and a safety hazard when driving on two wheels.

One day, major construction sent me on a detour, taking me five minutes out of my way. My first response to the construction and detour was frustration and annoyance.

"Ugh! This better not make me late to work," I thought.

> **Want more joy in life? Look for joy.**

Then I considered choosing an attitude of gratitude. "How can I be grateful in this moment?" I asked myself.

I smiled and laughed when I realized that the frustrating and annoying construction was repairing the road around the train tracks so I could enjoy a smoother and safer ride to work every day. It was a five-minute detour in exchange for a more pleasant daily experience!

Instead of arriving at work in an irritated and frenzied state, I arrived with gratitude and joy.

• •

Think of all the times you've adopted a negative attitude and how that small choice changed your experience of your day. What if you decided to adopt an attitude of gratitude instead? By considering the positive things happening around you, your perception of your daily life changes. As you practice gratitude, you start noticing more things to be grateful for.

The easiest way to build your gratitude muscle is to start a daily gratitude practice. Every day, make a list of what you're grateful for. Include everything from enjoying your favorite food, to finding a great parking spot, to having a roof over your head. Make note of the small stuff on your gratitude list, including the softness of your cat's fur, the cozy chair you curl up in to read a book, and the satisfying first sip of your morning coffee. Start with your five senses—be grateful for what you see, hear, taste, touch, and smell. Be intentionally grateful for all these things and more. If you're used to assuming the crash position, writing a gratitude list might be difficult at first. Make your daily list as long as you can and don't be afraid to include the little or obvious things, like being grateful for the people in your life or that the weather was good. Stick with the practice. When you write down your gratitude, it grows.

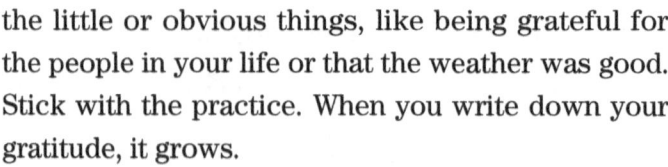

Keep up your daily gratitude practice for at least two weeks before looking for results. Then, see how long you can continue practicing gratitude daily. It took years to develop the capacity to see what could go wrong in every situation, so it will take practice to develop the capacity to notice all the things going right!

As you embark on your gratitude practice, experience the world with childlike wonder and notice all the amazing things around you. Add these things to your gratitude list. Develop your sense of play and whimsy. Be ridiculous and spontaneous and silly.

> **Develop your sense of play and whimsy.**

Now, there will be days when you're just not feeling it. Days when everything seems to be going wrong. Days when you're anxious and stressed and exhausted. Those days will be the hardest days to continue your gratitude practice, but they are the most important days to take the time to be grateful. Making a gratitude list on a shitty day can help you feel just a little bit better about your day. Your gratitude can give you perspective on what feels like a crappy day to help you identify when some things actually went right.

Here are some things that likely went right most days:

- You enjoyed a hot shower.
- A picture on your fridge reminded you of a happy memory.
- You enjoyed your morning cup of coffee.
- Your car started on the first try.

- You arrived at work safely.
- You had a choice of delicious foods to eat throughout the day.
- You were amused or comforted by a furry or feathered friend—maybe your cat, your dog, or a squirrel or bird you encountered outside.
- You enjoyed listening to a podcast or music, watching a show, or reading a book.
- You spoke to at least one person you love or, at the very least, like.
- You helped out someone else, positively impacting that person's day.
- You had someone to ask for help, even if you didn't specifically ask for help today.
- You had a comfortable, cozy place where you could rest—such as a favorite reading chair, a shady park bench under a tree, or your bed.
- If you had to, you could list at least five things you like about yourself.
- Someone showed you kindness today.

When your gratitude is recorded in a list, you can go back and revisit past gratitudes anytime you need a pick-me-up. So that shitty day when you're having a terrible time writing your gratitudes? Reread past lists. Gratitude can be a ray of hope on an otherwise shitty day.

Don't just take my word for it. The article "7 Scientifically Proven Benefits Of Gratitude That Will

Motivate You To Give Thanks Year-Round" by Amy Morin talks about the science around the health and wellness benefits of gratitude (Forbes.com, Nov 2014). She cites that gratitude fosters relationships, improves physical and mental health, enhances empathy, improves sleep and self-esteem, and increases resilience—all benefits I can attest to. But reading about the improvements isn't as convincing as experiencing them for yourself. I want you to know what I'm saying works because you try it for yourself.

> Remember, your direction follows your attention.

If you already have a regular gratitude practice, look for ways to go deeper.

- A fun exercise is to write a gratitude for every letter of the alphabet. Gratitude from A–Z! Everything from apples, affirmations, and animals to zippers, zeal, and 'za (pizza, that is!).

- Share your gratitude with others. Make your gratitude list public. I post my daily gratitude list on Facebook. Friends and acquaintances often comment on my gratitude list when I see them in person—it doesn't just inspire me, it inspires others, too. When you share your gratitude, it grows.

- Tell other people what you're grateful for—especially when you're grateful for them! Shower other people with compliments and you'll feel great. Start a regular compliment practice. Give three compliments every day for a week and see what happens. That's gratitude in action, my friends.

However you decide to practice gratitude, what's important is that you train your brain to look for what's going right. Soon enough you'll notice more and more things are going right, and your setbacks aren't as significant. If you experience depression or anxiety, a regular gratitude practice can improve your outlook. Remember, your direction follows your attention.

Random Acts of Self-Kindness

I'm a recovering perfectionist and I've always been hard on myself. From a very young age I believed I could and should be able to do anything I set my mind to.

I was two years old when my mom heard me screaming from my bedroom. She came rushing into the room, worried something was terribly wrong. She found me sitting on the floor with my tights tangled up around my little legs, screaming out of frustration because I was unable to put my tights on by myself, a task I was determined to do though I lacked the coordination to do so. I understood what needed to happen and hated that I couldn't do it myself.

When I was nine years old, I came home from school in tears. I came in through the front door, storming the front door, storming straight through the living room and into the kitchen. With great angst I angrily slammed a piece of paper in the trash bin. My mom watched the scene with some concern and inquired what I was throwing away.

> You do enough.
> You are enough.

"My homework! I failed!"

My mom reached in the trash and pulled out the paper. She stood there for a moment, surprised to see I had received a "B" grade.

"But, honey," she said, "you got a 'B.'"

"'B' is for bad," I replied.

I was the smallest, cruelest perfectionist.

> It's hard to be happy when someone is mean to you all the time, especially when that person is you.

Part of my journey was learning to be kind to myself. I could not see the ways in which I was gifted. I saw only where I fell short. My perfectionism contributed to the depression and anxiety I lived with from a young age. Overcoming my hardships and struggles required more compassion, more understanding, and more self-kindness. Healing needed forgiveness.

It's hard to be happy when someone is mean to you all the time, especially when that person is you. You may not even realize how mean you are to you. (Many of us don't.) I would never and could never be as cruel to others as I am to myself. I could never be so cruel to a child. Stop and think about it for a moment: Are you as kind to yourself as you are to a child?

Your own growth and healing is supported by kindness, compassion, and forgiveness. You're doing your best.

You do enough. You are enough.

To foster self-kindness, start by picturing yourself as a child and shift your thoughts and actions to her. It's much harder to be unkind to a child. Through her, you can find kindness and compassion for yourself. Imagine comforting the child version of you. Give her a hug or let her snuggle up to you. Hold her close and tell her she is loved. Ask her what she needs and give it to her. When you notice an unkind thought or word, forgive her, and in doing so, forgive yourself. Self-kindness takes practice, and daily forgiveness may be necessary.

A friend helped me understand that self-forgiveness is a powerful and necessary form of self-kindness. My friend was laid off and remained unemployed for many months. One day he said in front of me, "Today I forgive myself for not having a job."

This statement struck me deeply. I knew his frustrations and struggle seeking employment and was surprised by the way he articulated those frustrations with himself as forgiveness. After that experience, I adopted this idea. I began asking myself, "What do I need to forgive myself for today?" This simple question opened the door to kindness and compassion. I was reminded that I am doing enough. I am enough.

> What do you need to forgive yourself for today? What expectation is weighing you down? Forgive yourself for these things and more.

Learning to be kind to yourself is important when your habit is to be hard on yourself—and it's more important when you're going through a difficult time. Any time you're struggling, practice being extra kind to yourself and foster self forgiveness. Where you are right now is okay. Who you are right now is okay. You do enough. You are enough.

Choose Something Better

I grew up in the worst circumstances. I experienced poverty, abuse, domestic violence, addiction, and mental illness in my childhood home.

The first time I thought about suicide I was six years old.

Just a few months shy of my seventh birthday, I shut myself in the closet and cried. More than anything, I wanted to die. I had no real reason to think life would improve, no reason to think things would change, nevertheless I chose to live.

When I was eight years old, the night terrors began. Night after night I woke up screaming. Not knowing what else to do, my mother and stepfather took me to a psychiatrist who prescribed antidepressants. This was, of course, before antidepressants were as widely prescribed as they are today.

No one asked questions about the sexually transmitted disease I had contracted. No one seemed to connect it to my night terrors.

> **Day after day I found some reason, no matter how small, to keep living.**

Even after the antidepressants, it was the same every night—recurring dreams in which all of my family was killed and only I survived. In the dream, I would go to my parents' room and find them dead. A similar grisly scene awaited me in my older sister's room. When I ran to my baby sister's room, she was dead, too. Alone forever, forever alone. That's what he said would happen if I told anyone what he did to me—he would kill my family and I would be alone. I wanted to die, too.

Day after day I found some reason, no matter how small, to keep living. I chose to live.

One relatively normal day that same year, my alcoholic stepfather berated me, telling me I was worthless, I was shit—it was the same way he'd yelled at me many times before. He yelled and I cried. I was devastated. I thought about how much I hated my life, and how I longed to die. And then, something changed in me. It was a moment of conviction, a moment of hope.

In that moment, with tears streaming down my face, I decided I'd had enough. I was going to have a better life. With determination set on my face, I decided that when I grew up and could make my own choices, I was going to choose something better, something better than this.

At eight years old I didn't know how I would create this better life, but I knew I would find a way. I didn't know what I wanted, but I wanted something different than the life that had been given to me. From that moment on, I started pursuing something better.

Life didn't improve right away. In fact, it took a long time—a really long time—to actually feel better. And let's face it, I felt pretty shitty during that time. I was suicidal through my teens and into my early twenties. I suffered from depression and anxiety. I was diagnosed with post-traumatic stress disorder (PTSD). I struggled to get by.

Despite my feelings, I kept living. I kept trying. I never lost hope. I learned as much as I could from books and took advantage of whatever help or resources were available to me. I begged my mom to take me to Alateen, a support group for teens affected by alcoholism. I saw counselors at school. I found some relief in therapy.

I was open to trying just about anything to find the peace and happiness I believed was possible for me. Sometimes the people who provided resources were the most discouraging. Those well-meaning "good people" who were charitable and kind packaged their sympathy with pity. They looked down on me because I was poor and sad and fucked up. Those pitying people were harder to face than the ones who openly avoided or rejected me.

In high school I participated in a religion-based youth group. Like in most groups, I never quite felt like I fit in, but the weekly meetings were fun, so I went anyway. The group ran weekend and summer camps that offered scholarships for needy kids like me. I couldn't wait to go! About a week before summer camp, I overheard two of the group leaders talking about me. In concerned tones they voiced all of my fears—they didn't want me at camp because I didn't really fit in, but they didn't feel like they could turn me away.

Despite overhearing that conversation, I decided to go anyway. I went knowing I wasn't accepted or wanted—at least not by two of the people there. I didn't let that knowledge stop me.

I suppose that's been my mantra for most of my life—I won't let that stop me. I could have stayed home. I could have accepted pity. I could have believed my stepfather when he said I was worthless. I could have given up a hundred times over. But I didn't. I didn't let anything stop me. I put one foot in front of the other, day after day. I tried new things. I pushed myself outside my comfort zone. I challenged my beliefs about myself. I challenged other people's beliefs about me.

> I could have given up a hundred times over. But I didn't.

I kept trying to improve my situation. I couldn't rely on the examples set by my life and family. Those examples would only lead to repeating the life I'd already experienced. To make something better, I tried new things, sought out different experiences, and I made the most of my situation. Even when it was painful. Even when it was hard. I couldn't help what other people thought of me, but I could help what I did.

Eventually, it did get better. Not all at once. Little by little, it got better. I thought of dying less often. I felt less depressed. When I was eighteen, I moved out on my own and got a job, then a more desirable job, and a better job after that. I didn't have much, but I had more than I'd known for a long time.

It got worse again, too. It always does, doesn't it? But it never got as bad as it was, and even if it had, well, now I knew it could be better—I'd proven it. I made "better" happen before and I could make it happen again. I had believed a happier life was possible. I believed I could create something better. Because I believed in myself, I knew it could always improve.

I still feel like giving up all too often. I'm a high-achieving, recovering perfectionist. No wonder I feel like giving up. Sometimes I wish life were easy. Sometimes? I always wish that. But whenever I do, a thought pops into my brain: "it already is easy."

I'm far more comfortable with the idea that life is hard because that's what I know best. The idea that "life is easy" makes me uncomfortable as hell because "hard" is what I know and what has been reinforced. But when I trust in myself, when I believe things will change, when I'm no longer struggling just to survive, life can be easy, too. Instead of focusing on how hard things are, I can focus on the ease. The ease is always present somewhere—in the things I do well or that come naturally to me—but the hard things can be more obvious. How can I enjoy the things that are easy? How can I embrace and expand on that ease?

"Easy" may not be the word you would use, and maybe "easy" feels a long way off.

What I want you to know is that life can be better—so much better—better than anything you've known. You may eventually find that you think life is easy, too! The journey to find a better life is a worthy journey to take. You are worth that journey. As you continue on the path of growth, life will be hard and life will be easy. Believe both are possible as you begin to believe in you.

Believe in Yourself More than You Believe Others

Many women were raised to be the "good girl." Being the "good girl" might include putting the needs of others before your own, pleasing the most demanding family members, or doing as you're told. Too many women learn to believe what others tell them before believing themselves. Who are you listening to? Who do you believe more than you?

If your teacher said you're stupid, it must be true. If your coworker criticized your work, you must not be that good at your job. If your mother proclaimed you're arrogant, even years later you may avoid taking credit for your accomplishments to avoid anyone thinking you're full of yourself.

You, and only you, are responsible for your life. You're also the only one with the power to improve your life. You're the only one who really knows what's possible for you and how to make it happen. (You do know, even if it's buried deep.)

> You're the only one with the power to improve your life.

Throughout your life you will have teachers, mentors, confidants, and advisers, and their counsel will be invaluable. But other people may be ready to tell you what to think, feel, and believe. These people may be strangers, acquaintances, friends, or family members. They may be people you hate, or people you love. Don't listen to the wrong people.

Since you're the only one who can actually believe in yourself, it's important to recognize these naysayers when they come into your life. You have to consider if what they say is true about you and for you because not everyone will have your personal growth and support at heart. Knowing the right people to listen to will help you increase your belief in yourself and help you on the path to a better life.

Here are the top five people who will misguide you and how to respond to them. You may recognize someone in your life from one of these descriptions, so consider how you can change that relationship and support yourself.

1. The Chief Advantage Officer

My first husband was one example of the Chief Advantage Officer in my life. It served his interests to keep me small. He wanted to keep me close and would ask, bargain, and demand I give up more and more of who I am to give more and more to him.

The Chief Advantage Officer wants you to stay right where you are in life because they benefit from your position. It could be your boss, your significant other, or your friend. The Chief Advantage Officer gets more than he gives. He's looking out for his best interests first and foremost and, when it suits him, he will dump you without hesitation.

The Chief Advantage Officer prefers it when you're off-balance because you're easier to convince, manipulate, and control. He may swoop into your life when things are tough, and he doesn't really want you to be happy.

Ending the relationship with the Chief Advantage Officer is usually in your best interests.

2. The Mouse

A close family friend was the Mouse in my life. She cared for me deeply, and often cautioned me against testing my limits, pushing my boundaries, or getting too big for my britches. It took years for me to realize that her advice was overly cautious, based on her own fears and limiting beliefs.

The Mouse may be a family member or trusted friend. She means well and truly has your best interests at heart, but she is so afraid of personal risk, she will advise you to keep quiet, to play small, to live a mediocre life. It's hard not to listen to the Mouse because

you care about her, you know she cares about you, and you may also be afraid to take a risk.

The best method for dealing with the Mouse is to listen to her advice, but don't take it. You might respond to the Mouse's counsel by saying, "Thank you for your concern. I have a lot of choices to consider," or "hmmm… you've given me a lot to think about."

3. The Guru

I've come across many Gurus since starting my business. They are usually business consultants selling a product or service. They promise to teach me what I don't yet know how to do in my business, from marketing to sales to the right way to write my book. I am inundated with Facebook ads and carefully crafted lifestyle photos on Instagram from these Gurus, offering the right formula for success in six months or less! The Guru makes big assurances, based on their own formula for success. "If I can do it, so can you," the Guru asserts with confidence.

The Guru is knowledgeable and influential and may even help a lot of people. The problem is the Guru knows what worked for him and he assumes because it worked for him it will work for you, too. Ultimately, he believes he knows better than you because he is further along or more successful than you are. He doesn't appreciate or understand your unique circumstances, and because of this, he may give you bad counsel.

The Guru may be a boss, mentor, or coach, and he may be in the position you want, but it's important to consider if his advice makes sense for your situation. When it comes to the Guru, take what you like and leave the rest.

4. The Know-It-All

The Know-It-All is easy to identify by his expertise on any and every topic. One such example is a man who showed up at my women's leadership organization, She Goes High, and proceeded to direct the conversation at the table. When I introduced myself and explained that She Goes High is a group for women, he pronounced he was involved with many women's groups that allow men. He assured me he was "in charge of" an influential women's group and is an advocate for women. He seemed genuinely surprised when I took him up on his offer to leave. Surely he had all the answers—didn't I want to hear them? (Alas, I did not.)

The Know-It-All has all the answers—at least he thinks he does. The problem is he doesn't know what he's talking about! He likes to give advice to feel powerful and important, and he can be very convincing. He counsels with such confidence and self-assurance it's easy to believe what he says is true.

If you're discussing fictional wormholes, he suddenly has a degree in theoretical physics. He knows the best way to cook a chicken, is an expert on bike repair, and has plenty of advice to be successful in your career.

Avoid the Know-It-All if you can, and assume his opinion says more about him than it does about you!

5. The Codependent

I was the Codependent in certain relationships in my life. One relationship in particular was my codependent relationship with my mom, particularly through my teenage years. I was a good daughter—scratch that, I was the perfect daughter, or at least I tried to be. I wanted to be approved of, to be loved, and to prove that I was worth something. I wanted my mom's mental health to improve and being the dutiful daughter was a role I was happy to take on.

> Don't look back and see that you believed in other people more than you believed in yourself.

The Codependent shares traits with two of the other types, the Chief Advantage Officer and the Mouse. The Codependent is similar to the Chief Advantage Officer in that she benefits from her relationship with you—she defines her own worth in relation to you. Like the Mouse, the Codependent may also truly care about you and want what's best for you, though her idea of what's best may be clouded by her own interests. The Codependent benefits from feeling needed by you, and she may unconsciously keep you dependent on her.

The best defense against the Codependent is good boundaries. Say no when needed. Agree in advance to limits on your time and other resources. You may get some pushback since she benefits in some way from the relationship as it is. If the Codependent reacts negatively to those boundaries and tries to argue her way around them, instead of responding to every one of her arguments, speak to *your* truth. You don't have to attend every argument you're invited to.

If you want to believe in yourself, watch out for these five people in particular. These archetypes will tell you to trust them over yourself. They will tell you they know better than you. They will tell you not to believe in yourself—and they are wrong. At the end of your life, don't look back and see that you believed in other people more than you believed in yourself.

Self-Care: Beyond the Basics

Years of therapy, support groups, and self-help books taught me about the value of self-care. I learned to take better care of myself and felt justified in taking time for myself supported by the idea that "you can't pour from an empty cup."

Even so, I had a lot to learn about what self-care really means for me.

I thought I was pretty good at self-care, and still, I overcommitted and overextended myself. I suffered chronic health issues. I caught just about every cold going around. Despite my efforts at self-care, I burned myself out time and time again until I learned to stretch my self-care beyond the basics.

Most of the women I know understand the basics of self-care—taking care of your physical, mental, emotional, and spiritual health. Yet when push comes to shove, and so often it does, care for yourself is deemed a luxury instead of a priority. Women take care of themselves, sure, only it's *after* taking care of everyone else. *After* your work is done. *After* providing dinner for your family. *After* picking up groceries. "I'll just do this thing first. Okay, yeah, I'll get to my needs. In a minute."

> Women take care of themselves, sure, only it's after taking care of everyone else.

If you're going to create something epic and amazing with your life, you must take better care of yourself—especially if your normal is less than ideal or if you've survived with fewer resources than others.

Basic self-care includes:

- Eating regular healthy meals
- Getting an adequate amount of sleep
- A personal hygiene routine that may include washing your face, brushing your teeth, flossing, etc.
- A healthy emotional care routine that may include meditation, setting an intention for the day, journaling, gratitude lists, etc.
- Wearing clean, unwrinkled clothes that fit properly and feel good on you
- Exercising, including anything from enjoying a daily walk to a cardio workout
- Creating time for hobbies and other activities you enjoy

- Having and using a support network that may include family, friends, your therapist, a book club, etc.
- Taking time for yourself, especially if you're an introvert

....

When I started on this journey, even basic self-care was a challenge. I had lived most of my life just surviving, reacting to the latest crisis and fearing the next crisis on the horizon. I spent so much of my life in crisis I didn't know how to simply live day to day.

When my life was more stable and basic self-care was an easy part of my routine, I still had a problem. I rarely looked beyond caring for my basic needs and still was not addressing all my needs, especially in relation to other people. I would sacrifice sleep to stay up talking to a friend in crisis. I would spend too much of my limited grocery budget pitching in for a coworker's birthday lunch. I would overextend myself physically going on a difficult hike my boyfriend wanted to try.

I overlooked my other wants and needs in favor of people, obligations, and "shoulds." I "should" work late when asked. I "should" volunteer at a non-profit. I "should" prioritize attending my friend's art show. You may even do favors (that is, work for free) or take a loss to make a client happy because you feel like you "should."

Even trickier to navigate are those situations when you automatically default to someone else's best interests without stopping to consider your own. When you're so used to going from task to task, you rarely, if ever, stop to ask yourself why you're doing what you're doing. Bad habits can emerge when you're used to handling whatever comes next without much thought about why, or when you do things because you think you "should" and then let those obligations prevent you from taking care of yourself. Maybe you aren't even *considering* yourself as someone who also needs care.

Self-care goes beyond taking care of your health, it also includes fulfilling your wealth, which comes in the same physical, mental, emotional, and spiritual forms as health. It's going from surviving to thriving—to building the personal resources to live a better life.

Learning to advance my self-care took practice. I listened to therapists, support group peers, and friends talk about what they do for self-care. I stepped outside my self-care comfort zone, doing more for myself than I ever had before. To this day I continue to rediscover and redefine my care for myself. As I change, my needs change. Some days I need more care than others. When I'm under stress I know I need an extra dose of care.

• •

Advanced self-care includes:

- Saying no
- Setting boundaries at work and home
- Taking regular breaks throughout your workday
- Arriving and leaving work on time
- Not working for free
- Actively considering your best interests

- Acting in your best interests
- Believing in yourself
- Being selfish
- Being demanding
- Being intentional in all you do
- Speaking up for yourself
- Bragging about yourself
- Forgiving yourself for not being perfect
- Disappointing the right people
- Developing your intuition
- Raising your abundance limit, aka your internal glass ceiling
- Receiving compliments and praise with grace and ease
- Tuning in to your desire
- Following your dreams

Did you notice how many of these forms of self-care are included in this book? Yeah, that's right. This book is about taking care of you, because isn't about time someone did?

As you continue to read, and maybe even re-read this book, continue to challenge your idea of self-care. Go beyond the basics. Don't limit self-care to getting a manicure or going to bed early—it is those things and a lot more.

If you haven't mastered the basics of self-care, start there. Don't try to do it all at once. Pick one aspect of self-care to work on. Changing multiple habits at the same time (eating and sleep, for example) can be frustrating and lead to unclear results. Instead, let's say you start with sleep. Create boundaries around sleeping and work on your bedtime habits to create healthy habits that support a good night's rest. Try setting a bedtime alarm for an hour before bedtime. When the alarm goes off, put away electronic screens that can interfere with your sleep. Do some gentle stretches or take three full deep breaths to calm your mind and body. Create a bedtime routine that will relax and prepare you to get rest.

Whatever you try, focus on one goal for several weeks and celebrate your commitment and progress!

▶ When life interferes—and it will—refocus and keep putting your attention and intention on you. Yes, even when your boss or client emails you at 10:00 p.m. (Why were you checking your work email anyway?) Even when five minutes before bedtime your child asks for help with his homework. (Uh, that kid needs a good night's sleep, too, am I right?) You deserve a rich, full, and fulfilling life, and self-care is an important piece of enjoying a fulfilling life. Especially when you haven't always had it easy. Isn't it about time someone looks out for you? Start with you. Make yourself a priority. Easier said than done, I know. Remember, practice makes progress.

Radical Self-Love

When I was eleven or twelve years old, my mom read a self-help book that changed the course of my life. That book was *Women Who Love Too Much: When You Keep Wishing and Hoping He'll Change* by Robin Norwood. Because of this book my mom began counseling and attending Al-Anon, a support group for families of alcoholics.

At twelve years old I didn't understand what Al-Anon was, but it helped my mom and I thought maybe it could help me, too. When I made the decision to create a better life for myself, I knew it would involve learning new ways to cope—ways that were different from the examples set for me by my family. I begged my mom to take me to Al-Anon, and soon I began attending Alateen, part of Al-Anon Family Groups, focused on helping teens cope with alcoholism in the family.

Each week, we sat on mismatched chairs around a scratched up table in an upstairs bedroom of an old house. The room smelled like stale cigarettes and old coffee. We drank out of chipped mugs and we shared our experience, strength, and hope. In those rooms, I began to create the better life I wanted. In those rooms, I first learned about powerlessness, detachment with love, and self-love. Alateen was the first support group I discovered, and to this day I practice the principles I learned in Alateen.

I had only been to a few meetings when I heard a woman sharing about practicing self-love. She looked at herself in the mirror every day and said, "I love you." She said when she first tried this self-love practice, it felt ridiculous and strange. It was uncomfortable. She wanted to look away.

Self-love was a foreign idea to me, but I was desperate. I wanted to feel better. I wanted to be happier. What did I have to lose? I was willing try her practice of saying "I love you" in the mirror.

So I did it. Every day for two weeks I looked at myself in the mirror, staring into my pale blue eyes framed by blonde curls, and said, "I love you." As suggested, this ritual was awkward and alien. I squirmed with discomfort and my gaze darted away from my reflection. Every time I said "I love you" to myself, my mind immediately retorted more familiar comments: "You're hard to love." "You're worthless." "You'll never be good enough."

I had heard those words of hate so many times before. I first heard them from the withered mouth of my grandmother and from my seething stepfather. I heard those hurtful words so many times that I started to believe them and started saying them to myself. Those words were my knee-jerk reaction to any expression of love. In order to accept love, I guess I had to say "I love you" a hundred times to myself before I started to really believe I was lovable with the same conviction I believed I was unlovable.

I continued to look in my own eyes and say, "I love you." I said it every day for months, and then for many months more. As I had slowly learned to believe the hateful comments directed at me, through this radical self-love practice I slowly began to believe I was worthy of love. I began to feel love and compassion for myself. With time I could say these words without trembling, without immediately looking away.

After my initial success talking to myself in the mirror, I began another self-love practice. After so many years of negative self-talk, I began to practice positive

> You are worthy.
> You are lovable.

self-talk. The first step was noticing when I said negative statements about myself. Thoughts are powerful and words spoken aloud carry even more power. I practiced only *thinking* negative words instead of speaking them. Soon thereafter, I began to speak aloud two positive statements for every negative thought. Over the course of several months I noticed an increase in my positive self-talk and a decrease in my negative self-talk and self-thoughts. Shifting my self-talk to the positive made it easier to love myself. I was worthy of love and I loved myself.

Learning radical self-love was one of the very first gifts I received from Alateen. It didn't matter where I came from, who I was, or what I had done. I was, and am, worthy of love.

Self-love doesn't always come easy. Too often you've been told you were wrong. You've been told exactly how you screwed up. You've been dismissed and treated with disrespect. And at some point in your life you began to believe you must have done something to deserve this treatment. You began to believe you aren't worthy of love, or you're only worthy of a lesser form of love.

I'm here to tell you that you are good and beautiful and whole. You are worthy. You are lovable. If you don't believe me, start talking to yourself in the mirror. What do you have to lose? What do you have to gain?

Overcoming Self-Doubt

I don't know anyone who doesn't experience self-doubt. Why is this experience so universal? What is self-doubt, really?

I believe most self-doubt begins in childhood, but these foundational experiences might continue or occur in adulthood. Some common causes of self-doubt include:

- Being criticized as a child by a parent, teacher, or trusted advisor
- Being told not to trust our feelings or experiences by a parent, teacher, trusted advisor, or spouse (includes gaslighting)
- Being rejected or excluded
- Being a minority and/or having a minority opinion
- Being a visionary with ideas that challenge the status quo

Whatever the cause, self-doubt affects your ability to trust yourself. It's the thought that everyone else knows better than you—even when the subject matter *is* you. If no one

> If no one expects much from you, it's hard to believe you can amount to much.

expects much from you, it's hard to believe you can amount to much.

Self-doubt is the feeling that you aren't enough. You're not good enough. Not smart enough. Not pretty enough. Just not enough.

Many people experience self-doubt in the form of impostor syndrome. Often defined as the fear of being found out as a fraud, impostor syndrome is the result of your inability to integrate your accomplishments and achievements. It happens when you believe your success is the result of luck, timing, and/or deception. It presents as not believing you've earned your success.

I've spent my life trying to prove myself. I grew up poor. I suffered from anxiety and depression. My family members were not the most accomplished. I was used to being looked down on and thought of as less than—less fortunate, less able, less desirable.

I was lucky to have one person who believed in me no matter what. Someone who believed I could do anything I wanted to do. Someone who believed I was worthy. That person was me. Even during the times of my life when I wanted to die, when I was depressed and taking antidepressants, some small part of me believed I was worthy. I trusted myself. I believed in myself despite my circumstances. And I still experienced self-doubt.

Overcoming Self-Doubt

So many times I felt like an impostor. (Especially around writing this book!) Self-doubt shows up for me when I'm afraid to push forward. Yet somehow I find I'm not really afraid of failing—I'm far more afraid of succeeding. The idea of success feels foreign because I wasn't raised to believe I could have a happy and successful life. The seed of self-doubt that was planted in my childhood grew into a sour fruit that is more comfortable with failure.

At some point in my past I adopted the belief that if the world is separated into the haves and the have-nots, I'm a have-not. I didn't *have* things or *have* love or *have* success because *having* was not for me. I was predestined to *not have* and it wasn't something I could change. This idea helped me cope with the stark reality of my situation at its worst. The idea that I wouldn't amount to much was actually a little bit comforting. It meant I didn't have to keep trying. It meant I'm not really all that special and I can find comfort in living the rest of my life in mediocrity.

But the belief that I was a have-not, that I wasn't good enough or that I couldn't have what I desired, was a lie. That lie kept me from trying to reach beyond the middle of the pack. It kept me earning a modest salary at

Beautiful Badass

a modest job, driving a modest car, living a modest life. When I could have had more, it kept me mediocre. I was and still am lured into believing that lie, even when that lie directly conflicts with what I know to be true. I am enough. I am good enough. I am a have, not a have-not.

> Overcoming self-doubt is really about trusting yourself.

One of my favorite quotes comes from author Marianne Williamson: "Our deepest fear is not that we are inadequate. Our deepest fear is that we are powerful beyond measure. It is our light, not our darkness that most frightens us. We ask ourselves, who am I to be brilliant, gorgeous, talented, fabulous? Actually, who are you not to be?"

Indeed, who am I not to be fabulous? Who are you?

So, what does it take to truly overcome self-doubt? Overcoming self-doubt is really about trusting yourself. It doesn't mean taking courageous action with confidence; it's taking courageous action *with* self-doubt. Overcoming self-doubt is choosing to believe in yourself even when you have doubts.

The Seed of Self-Worth

How do you believe in yourself? This was the hardest part of this book to write because while there are steps you can take to build your belief in yourself, you have to act as if you believe in yourself before you feel it, and sometimes that's very difficult to do.

Imagine that there is a seed inside of you. This seed is inherent in all life—it's the spark of life. It is incorruptible, but it requires nourishment. This is the foundation of self-worth. The seed of self-worth is inside me simply because I exist, not because of what I've done or who I am. It is not a conscious construct. It is not a thought, idea, or choice. It simply is. The seed of self-worth confirms I am worthy of life.

As I created a better life for myself, nourishing myself and tending to the seed of self-worth, it grew and eventually matured. Other seeds that were planted in my childhood, the seed of self-doubt and the hateful words I heard again and again, threatened to choke the growth of self-worth, but as I continued to care for the seed of self-worth, my self-worth flowered and bloomed.

The seed of self-worth is inside you, too. You wouldn't have survived this long if you didn't have at least a little self-worth. The seed may be buried deeply—and I can't tell you how to find the seed of self-worth inside of you—but I can assure you it *is* inside you and you *need* that seed to grow your self-worth.

> **If you don't already, you'll begin to believe that you can do amazing things. (You can.)**

Once you find your seed—the belief that you're worth nurturing—you water it, you feed it, you give it sunshine and love, and it grows. The more it grows, the more you'll see, feel, and believe in yourself. With nourishment, your little seed of self-worth will burst from underground, unfolding its leaves as it stretches into the sun. If you don't already, you'll begin to believe that you can do amazing things. (You can.) You'll begin to believe you're worthy. (You are.) You'll begin to believe it can get better from here. (It can.)

Believing in yourself isn't an all or nothing road. Sometimes you won't believe in yourself. Sometimes you'll question if you're really worth it. Welcome to humanity. It's normal to question yourself from time to time. Sometimes it's difficult to nurture that seed of self-worth when you don't believe that it will ever bloom, but that's the time when it's most important to turn garbage into fertilizer. Do it messy. Do it imperfectly. Do it little by little, day by day.

There are a million different ways to nurture your seed. You nurture it with self-care, self-love, and self-kindness. You must tend to it every day. Every day, choose to do at least one thing that shows yourself, and the world, that you believe in yourself.

You show yourself that you believe in yourself when you're scared, anxious, or depressed. You show yourself that you believe in yourself when you're brave, excited, or joyful. Every day you show yourself you believe in yourself when you stretch outside your comfort zone, when you challenge your past experience, and when you act as if you believe in yourself, even when you're just starting the journey to healing your life.

Here are four steps to nurture your seed of self-worth:

1. Read this book. (Hooray, you've already started!)

    Pick a practice in this book and do it consistently for two weeks. Notice how you feel. Notice what you experience. If it works for you, keep doing it! If it doesn't work, pick a different activity in this book and do it consistently for two weeks. Repeat until you discover a solution that supports you.

2. If this book doesn't work for you, pass it on to someone else. Pick another book, podcast, or resource for yourself. *Find something that does work for you.*

3. Keep going. Don't worry about getting it right, just get it!

Treat yourself as if you are worthy and you *are* worthy. Act as if you believe in yourself and you believe. Give your seed love and attention and it grows. The spark is inside you and ready to be cultivated. All you have to do is believe.

How to Believe in Yourself When Things Aren't Going Well

Like many of the ideas in this book, believing in yourself is a bit of a paradox. It is the hardest—and the easiest—thing to do.

When you've had to struggle and fight and overcome, you might believe it's your fault that you wound up in that situation—that you must have done something to deserve your lot in life. Maybe someone even told you it was your fault: "You didn't work hard enough." "You didn't want it enough." "You weren't good enough." (Lies.)

It's not your fault, so give yourself a break! Better even, give yourself some credit. You've had to struggle and fight and overcome. Look at all you've been through. Look at the incredible person you are. You, my friend, are one incredible, resilient, amazing, resourceful, brave human being. (Not lies.)

The hard part of believing in yourself is challenging old thoughts and beliefs. The stories you were told when you had it hard, when you tried and failed, when you didn't feel as good as everyone else seemed to, formed the foundation of your self-image, and you have to challenge that image to be able to believe in yourself. Other people will always have lots of opinions about what you think and say and do. One tip for challenging their beliefs is to remember that other people's opinions of you are none of your business. Let me repeat that: Other people's opinions of you are none of your business. Changing your actions to change someone's opinion isn't effective. At the end of your life there's only one person you can please, and that person is you. Stop changing yourself for the sake of other people's opinions, and start believing in yourself just for you.

> Say to the world, and to yourself, "I believe in me."

It's easier to believe in yourself when things are going well. When you've just been hired in an exciting new job, or when you sign your first client, or when you start a new relationship, everything seems possible. But what about those times when things aren't going well? When you've been unemployed for months and your savings are running low, or when you have zero clients and the mortgage is due, or when you just ended a relationship that you thought was "the one"? In times like these it's harder to believe in what is possible. It's harder to trust. It's harder to believe in yourself.

If you can't believe in yourself today, start by acting as if you do believe in yourself. Say to the world, and to yourself, "I believe in me." Here are some ideas to get you started.

Align Your Behavior with Your Values

Your values are the beliefs about your work and your life that guide your purpose. You might value personal health, community, honesty, development, personal wealth, or business profitability. Whatever you believe in, your core values inform your sense of self.

When you believe in what you're doing, you believe in yourself. If, on the other hand, your actions are at odds with your core values, you can lose faith in yourself at the first sign of rejection.

How often do you act against your core values to please someone else? Doing so can result in a loss of faith in self. For example, if you value honesty and a friend asks you to lie for them, it's totally okay to tell your friend you're not comfortable lying on their behalf. Acting in line with your values builds trust and faith in yourself.

Align Your Choices with Your Intentions

Intentions are the desired results of your actions—think of them like goals. For example, if your goal is to live a healthy life, it's important to make choices that support that goal. Eating a gallon of ice cream would not be an aligned choice. (But definitely eat ice cream! Just, you know, one scoop, or maybe two.)

When your choices are aligned with your intentions, it's easier to believe in yourself because you're clear about where you're headed.

Discover Other Sources of Support

If no one you know supports your dreams and ideas, you can choose to look elsewhere for support and encouragement. If your mom doesn't "get it," stop talking to your mom about your dream career. You can talk to your mom about other stuff.

Find people who are working toward similar goals and build relationships with people who share your values and intentions. It's easier to believe in yourself when you share your purpose and progress with people who are on a related path. Find your people.

Tell Yourself You Can

The way you treat yourself has a significant impact on your belief in yourself. Be mindful of the messages you think and say about yourself.

If you tell yourself you can't do it, it's likely you won't be able to because you already expect to fail. Tell yourself you can do it. Better yet, look at yourself in the mirror and say, "I believe in you!" (Does this sound familiar? That's because the mirror exercise is useful for all kinds of positive support.)

Fear can also be a message you're sending yourself. If you

are too afraid to try, you're telling yourself you don't believe you will succeed. Taking even one small step despite your fear declares that you believe in you!

Always Do Your Best

When you know you tried your best, it matters less if things don't work out the way you wanted. You know there was nothing you could have done better, and you have the opportunity to learn from the situation and improve. Don't beat yourself up! Give yourself mad props for doing the best you could at the time. Each setback is a building block for future success.

> Those old patterns, those old beliefs, they don't serve you anymore, and maybe they never did.

If you didn't do your best before, do it now. Every moment is a chance to try something new, to practice being the best version of you.

Celebrate Your Accomplishments

If you focus too intently on achieving your goal, you might find it harder to believe in yourself before you reach your goal. You and I both know how that goes. Sometimes the goal is a long way off, and sometimes even when you reach your goal, it's somehow still not good enough.

Instead, celebrate your accomplishments and milestones along the way! Acknowledging your progress builds your confidence. You're on your way—keep up the good work! Celebrating small successes builds confidence and faith, leading to more and more success.

Hopefully this is all starting to sink in and maybe you're noticing shifts in your thoughts and behaviors. If so, it means you are replacing those patterns of thinking and doing that were the result of surviving. Those old patterns, those old beliefs, they don't serve you anymore, and maybe they never did. They had their place in your past, and their place is not here, not now, not today.

Don't Quit Before the Miracle

When I was eight years old, there was a story contest at school. I sat on the living room floor, casually flipping through a magazine, trying to come up with a good story idea.

As I turned the page, I sneezed on a car advertisement. "Cars are lucky they don't have so many problems," I mused. "They don't have allergies, either."

My great story idea was born and I wrote my story about a car that was allergic to gas. On the heels of three movies about a self-aware 1963 Volkswagen Bug named Herbie, I imagined the car in my story to be a yellow Beetle.

The story opened with the car sneezing violently, using his windshield wipers to clear his watery, red windshield eyes. His entire yellow body was covered in

itchy red spots. Having tried every type and brand of fuel he could find, searching the world as far as his wheels would take him, the car was distraught and depressed to discover he was allergic to every brand and type of fuel. He was miserable.

The yellow Bug with splotchy red spots and bright red, irritated eyes was so depressed he decided to take his own life. On his last tank of gasoline he prepared to carry out his suicide.

"I will drive off the top of the Empire State Building," he resolved. He set off on his last drive to the Empire State Building. Upon arriving, he was displeased to discover he was too big to fit in the elevator, and he was well over the weight limit!

His next suicide plan was less dramatic. He decided to drown himself in the ocean. He drove to the shore and approached the dock. As he began to roll down the dock, hearing the thump-thump, thump-thump of his wheels on the wooden slats, he suddenly realized he was terrified of sharks! He had, of course, seen the 1975 blockbuster movie *Jaws*. He was willing to drown, but he didn't want to die from a shark attack. With resignation he gave up on his plan to commit suicide that day.

Forlorn that his suicide attempts had been thwarted, he settled on driving back to his garage and rusting away in the cold and dark for the rest of his life. He would never again see the sun, drive along a country road, or take his beloved passengers where they needed to go. He would sit and wait to die.

On his way back to his garage, he spotted a thin old man in a black suit, sitting with a suitcase on the side of the road. The car wondered if the man needed help, and stopped to offer the man some assistance. After all, he might as well make the most of his very last drive.

The old man gratefully accepted a ride, loaded his suitcase in the backseat, and climbed into the car. He had a kind face with a groomed white beard. The man noticed the car seemed unwell and inquired, "What's the matter, son?"

The car regaled the man with his tale of woe, feeling a bit better having shared his pain. When they arrived at the man's destination, a quaint two-story house, the car bid him goodbye and thanked the man for listening. The man graciously thanked the car for the ride and wished him well.

A few miles down the road, on the last few drops of gas on his very last tank, practically running on fumes, the car pulled into his garage. It had been a very upsetting day, and the car closed his eyes with an exhausted sigh and promptly fell asleep.

The next morning the car woke, bright and early, his fuel gauge reading empty. Out of habit, he started up for the day, and somehow, despite having no fuel in his tank, he could start his engine! He turned on his headlights and honked his horn. Beep beep! It was a miracle! He could drive without gas!

The car was overjoyed and went about his life as he'd always wanted to live. He took long drives down winding roads, through the hustle and bustle of city traffic, all while driving happy and misery-free!

Several weeks later, on one of these casual drives about town, the car saw the old man in the black suit, once again sitting on the side of the road. The car was enthusiastic to see him because all this time he'd been carrying the man's suitcase. The car pulled over and offered the man a ride.

The man opened the door and sat in the passenger seat. The car explained, "I can run without fuel! It's a miracle! Ever since that day I first gave you a ride. Since then I've been looking for you on my drives. You left your suitcase in the backseat."

It was then that the old man explained the black box he had been carrying was no ordinary suitcase. In fact, it was a solar powered panel that allowed the car to run on solar energy instead of gas. He hadn't forgotten his suitcase after all, it had been a gift.

. . . .

I won the story contest with my story about the car who was allergic to gas. Writing this story at eight years old I often thought about suicide. Like the car, I was miserable. I was depressed. I suffered from circumstances beyond my control. The thought of ending my suffering was a welcome reprieve.

Despite my circumstances, I had hope. Enough hope to believe that there was another way out of suffering.

Enough hope to believe that somehow, somewhere, some kind stranger might offer me some comfort and give me a gift that would turn my life around.

I can't sell you the steps to believing in yourself, but I can tell you that the first step will likely be small. That step might be sharing your pain with a counselor or friend. That step might be making a plan to change the parts of your life that cause your suffering. It might be buying and reading a book that inspires you. Each small step you make will lead to the next step and the next step and the next. These progressive steps are not only how you strengthen your belief in yourself, they're also how you build your confidence. Do something every day that scares you. Seek out new ideas and experiences. All of those daily small steps added together allow you to make significant progress and travel a great distance.

> Each small step you make will lead to the next step and the next step and the next.

Sometimes you might be ready to a take a big, scary step. A step like leaving a job you hate, investing in your future, getting up on stage in front of hundreds of people, or writing a book. Sometimes you take a big, scary step, and then a series of small steps. The size of your steps will vary, but they're all forward progress.

Keep challenging yourself. Keep taking steps—small and large. Keep encouraging yourself and believing anything is possible. Keep believing in yourself, even when you don't feel like it. Don't give up on yourself before your solar-powered solution. Don't quit before your miracle.

> *I know that many men and even women are afraid and angry when women do speak, because in this barbaric society, when women speak truly they speak subversively—they can't help it: if you're underneath, if you're kept down, you break out, you subvert. We are volcanoes. When we women offer our experience as our truth, as human truth, all the maps change. There are new mountains.*
>
> *That's what I want—to hear you erupting. You young Mount St. Helenses who don't know the power in you—I want to hear you.*

Ursula K. Le Guin
Bryn Mawr College Commencement Address, 1986

Part 2:
Courage

What do I want?

Courage is necessary for the woman who puts other people's interests before her own. It is necessary for the woman who plays small, doing great work but not so great as to be publicly acknowledged for that work. Courage is necessary for the high-achieving woman doing all the work behind the scenes while other people get the credit, for the woman trying to take up as little space as possible in the world, for the woman who doesn't want to step on anyone's toes, for the woman who has been told she isn't good enough and believes it.

If you identify with any of these descriptions, and if you feel you lack the courage to change those things, this section is for you. On the left is a little encouragement to get things rolling.

Divorced and Bankrupt at Twenty-Nine

Nineteen years ago I sat alone in a limousine, my white dress gathered around me, my makeup carefully applied. Listening to Tori Amos, I cried as I told the driver to circle the block one more time. My tears weren't tears of joy, nor were they tears of sadness. I cried simply because I couldn't believe I was getting married. I never imagined *I* would get married. I didn't deserve happiness. For much of my life I didn't believe I deserved love. Getting married challenged my deepest, darkest beliefs about myself.

My relationship with my first husband was the best relationship I had known. It was healthier and happier than the relationships I saw modeled as a child. My husband was handsome with a stocky frame, dark shiny hair, and kind eyes. He was incredibly thoughtful and compassionate. He often lavished me with gifts and tokens of his love. He was exceedingly kind to animals. He was doting and considerate. He was fun.

My husband loved me, so maybe I wasn't unlovable after all.

A few months after my tearful wedding day, I started to see the cracks in the relationship. One Saturday I spent the day at a local science fiction convention, meeting celebrities, hearing behind-the-scenes stories of movies and shows I loved, shopping for collectibles, and forming new friendships with people who shared my love of *Star Trek* and *Buffy the Vampire Slayer*. It was one of my favorite events to attend each year.

When I came home with stories and pictures of my exciting meeting with *Buffy the Vampire Slayer* actor Nicholas Brendon, my husband was furious with me.

"It's unacceptable for you to be gone all day," he fumed. "We're married now. You shouldn't leave the house for more than three hours other than going to work." He explained that as a married couple we had devoted our lives to each other and that meant forsaking everyone and everything outside the marriage. He was mine and I was his—that was our vow.

I sat on the couch, flabbergasted by his outrageous demands. "I'm an independent woman, and I'm going to do what I want," I said defiantly. He stood there, looking at me, presumably waiting to see if I would back down. I didn't.

At the time, I thought speaking up for myself was enough. I didn't realize this was the beginning of a pattern to isolate and control me: early warning signs of domestic violence.

My husband never physically harmed me, and I thought that meant things were okay. I didn't know his attempts to control my behavior and tell me I was stupid were abuse. I didn't know this pattern of control and manipulation was a precursor to the physical and sexual violence I grew up with.

As happens in most abusive relationships, I didn't realize I was in one until it was too late.

Yet all along I knew *something* was wrong. My husband was jealous. He was depressed and deeply unhappy, and so was I. As his depression deepened, his controlling behavior escalated. He insisted I quit my Saturday morning adult jazz dance class. (I didn't.) He resented the two hours every Tuesday I spent watching *Buffy the Vampire Slayer* and *Angel*, whining and complaining about anything that took my attention away from him. (I kicked him out of the living room and watched what I wanted.) He demanded I come straight home after work instead of joining my coworkers for a matinee at the local movie theater. (I went anyway.)

> I reveled in my rebellion. He would try to control me and I wasn't having it!

I reveled in my rebellion. He would try to control me and I wasn't having it!

Despite the problems in our marriage, things were going well in both our careers. My husband started a new job at a tech company with a big signing bonus and a generous salary. I was hired by a different tech company with tons of employee perks, including free snacks, great benefits, and catered breakfast at our weekly staff meeting.

Bolstered by our professional success, we moved to a newly remodeled apartment with a washer/dryer in the unit and two balconies with an impressive view of the Rocky Mountains. I bought my very first car at the age of twenty-five.

When the dot-com bubble burst in 2000, we were laid off from our respective jobs within 24 hours of each other. My career bounced back quickly. Within two months I found another job, though I was earning $7,000 less than my previous inflated salary.

My husband struggled to find employment. His job experience and skills as a software engineer, in high demand just a few months earlier, were suddenly useless. After ten months of unemployment and an unsuccessful stint in bartending school, my husband eventually landed an entry-level office job through a temp agency.

Finally we were both employed again, but the peace of mind didn't last long. My mother-in-law called, asking about the insistent collections calls and letters she was getting. "They call every day," she said, exasperated. "I'm so stressed. Please give them your correct contact information."

I was shocked to learn my husband had multiple overdue accounts listed at his mother's address and phone. After so many months of unemployment, our financial situation was already strained. To learn of secret accounts was a complete betrayal.

"It's none of your business," he insisted when I confronted him. "It has nothing to do with you."

I had asked him to go to marriage counseling with me many times before. It wasn't until his hidden past-due debts were revealed that he relented. We sat stiffly next to each other on the couch in the counselor's office. The distance between us was palpable though we sat only inches apart. For a few months we went through the motions, barely communicating between counseling appointments. I knew we couldn't repair the marriage—there wasn't enough relationship to repair.

Our marriage was crumbling, and it took almost a year before I asked for a separation, and then later for a divorce. I saw divorce as proof that I couldn't make marriage work because I wasn't good enough. Divorce felt like the ultimate failure. I failed as a wife. I failed as a person. Divorce proved my deepest, darkest fear was true—I was inherently unlovable.

Despite my failure, after so many years of therapy and pursuing the better life I promised myself, I *had* learned to love myself (even if I still thought no one else could). When I finally harnessed my determination and made the decision to leave my marriage, I made that choice out of self-love. In allowing myself to fail at marriage, I acted with great courage, compassion, and love. Allowing myself to fail at my miserable marriage was a success.

A few years later, still reeling from the financial fallout of my divorce, I failed again. Wanting a fresh start, I moved to Fort Collins, about seventy miles north of Denver. Fort Collins had everything I loved about Denver— fresh Colorado air, mountain views, and a relaxed Colorado vibe.

> Choosing divorce and bankruptcy were two of the best choices I had made in my life.

I found a great job. I was rebuilding my life and it was starting to get good again, but my financial situation remained bleak. During the separation and divorce I had been able to make minimum payments on all my accounts every month, yet I realized how little I had to show for it. I lived a lifestyle not too far above the poverty I grew up with.

My situation was worse than I wanted to admit. One night at my girlfriend's house, the kitchen smelling of cleaner, I reached across the counter to get a glass from the cabinet. Too late, I noticed the counter was still wet. As I pulled back, a noticeable bleach-stain appeared on my favorite pair of dress pants. I ran to the bathroom and futilely tried to wipe away the stain. I came out of the bathroom and sat on the stairs, sobbing as she tried to console me. I couldn't afford to buy new pants. All my money was going to cover the debt from my failed marriage. In that moment I realized the absurdity of my situation—crying over a pair of ruined pants. I couldn't continue to live like this.

My situation got worse when I snapped my pinky finger in half and underwent two hand surgeries and twelve weeks of physical therapy. Even with a good job and medical insurance, the medical bills amounted to more than I could afford.

Here I was, approaching thirty, saddled with medical and marital debt, with no financial assets. As I took stock of my situation, I realized I could continue to live just above the poverty line, diligently paying my bills, and I wouldn't pay off all my debts until I was almost forty.

Deciding to file for bankruptcy was almost as painful as deciding to get divorced. Again, I was a failure. I was a loser. I was worthless. And somehow I knew that making the choice to file for bankruptcy was the most self-loving and self-affirming choice I could make. In fact, if I really hated myself that much, I would have just continued to be poor and cry over ruined pants.

I filed for bankruptcy and started over financially. I filed for divorce and started over in love. Twice in my life I failed, making the scary decision to publicly admit my failure. Twice I made painful yet loving decisions that supported my best future. Choosing divorce and bankruptcy were two of the best choices I had made in my life.

Disappointing the Right People

Raise your hand if you're a people-pleaser. (Try not to drop the book as you throw your hand in the air.) I have a bad habit of people-pleasing, and I have to tell you, it's gotten me nowhere good. In an effort to please everyone, I burned myself out. I took responsibility for problems and situations that weren't mine. I overcommitted myself time and time again. I took on too much.

Let's be honest, it wasn't just that I took on too much. Trying so hard to be everything to everyone meant that I wasn't able to be Really Amazing at any one thing. Instead, I was Pretty Good at a lot of different things but not even necessarily the things I wanted to be good at.

As a young professional I became the office helper—willing to drop everything and help everyone and anyone else at a moment's notice. I taught myself how to fix problems with copier and fax machines, I could troubleshoot software glitches like a pro, oh, and of course I covered the phones while a coworker took a break. Eventually all this helping meant I struggled to get my own work done.

Taking on too much also became a way to play small, another defense mechanism. By playing small I didn't have to find out just how amazing my life could be if I went after what I really wanted. If I wasn't going after just one goal—focusing on doing one thing (like my job) really well—I couldn't be too successful. I was so busy doing everything for everyone else, I wasn't doing much for myself. I still managed to create a certain level of success for myself, but my people-pleasing definitely held me back.

In the process of overgiving, I knew I disappointed people—most of all me. I considered my interests last, only after I knew other people were taken care of. But, in a codependent relationship, when are other people really taken care of? Especially when I encouraged the other person to come to me with problems—no problem too big or too small!

In the end, it wasn't just me that suffered, my closest relationships suffered, too. I found it was imperative to appease coworkers, acquaintances, and even strangers over the people closest to me. On some level I suppose I knew, or at least hoped, my family and friends would forgive me for letting them down even as I tried so

Disappointing the Right People

hard to let no one down. My family and friends loved me, and I was so desperate to get everyone's approval that I spent far more of my energy trying to please new people rather than being there for friends and family and, most of all, myself.

Ouch.

In 2012 I attended BlissDom, a conference for bloggers. BlissDom was an inspiring, engaging, multi-day educational event held at the Gaylord Opryland Hotel in Nashville, Tennessee. The keynote presentation was a startling challenge to my people-pleasing behavior. That day, sitting in the ballroom, surrounded by hundreds of strangers and soon-to-be friends, bestselling author Jon Acuff introduced me to a whole new idea—disappointing the right people.

Jon told a story about paying more attention to his Twitter followers than this daughter. His daughter needed help studying for a spelling test. As Jon interacted with his followers, his daughter became frustrated. She handed him a note written on a napkin, "Daddy, pay atenchun!" Jon's message was to choose who you disappoint, and that it's important to disappoint the right people. Who are the right people? You decide. Will you disappoint your Twitter followers or your daughter? Will you disappoint your coworker or your spouse? Will you disappoint your disapproving Aunt Ethel or yourself? You're going to disappoint someone—who's it going to be?

Listening to Jon's keynote speech, I realized how often I was responding to whomever was in front of me, instead of being intentional about my choices. Like Jon, I was often disappointing the people who were most important, and the person I disappointed most often was me.

> By trying to please everyone, I please no one because people have problems I cannot solve.

Being a people-pleaser doesn't mean I actually please anyone. Let's face it, people are hard to please. By trying to please everyone, I please no one because people have problems I cannot solve. For years I had tried to make things better for my mom, but I never had the power to make things better for her. I didn't cause her mental illness. I couldn't control her mental illness. I couldn't cure her mental illness. I could only make things better for me. The only person I can truly please is me.

It's okay to disappoint the acquaintance who invited you out for coffee. It's okay to disappoint the friend who hasn't bothered to reach out to you in months. It's even okay to disappoint your boss. (Yes, I promise it's okay.) Sometimes it's okay to disappoint your friends and family. It's even okay to disappoint yourself. What's important is making intentional choices about who, how, and when you disappoint so that you disappoint the right people for a good reason instead of unintentionally disappointing the wrong people.

A great way to put this idea into action is to ask yourself, "Who am I willing to disappoint today?" It can be scary to think of disappointing anyone, let alone accepting that disappointment is a normal part of life, and then choosing to disappoint the right people. If you're going to disappoint someone no matter what, don't you want to be intentional about who you'll disappoint?

Stop Comparing Yourself to Others

Growing up, I lacked healthy, successful adult role models. I had limited financial security and I struggled with PTSD, anxiety, and depression. I didn't have the same opportunities or advantages as my peers, and, as a result, when I compared myself to those around me, I could never measure up. They were the haves and I was a have-not. I was jealous of everything they had that I didn't.

This jealousy was particularly prevalent in my high school years. I attended an affluent school, sharing my classes with the children of state Senators, the heirs to the third-largest brewing company in the world, and other kids whose parents owned local businesses and were otherwise successful. My high school garnered the nickname "white rich high school," which was true for many students, but not for me. I was one of very few students at my school who lived in poverty and participated in the National School Lunch Program, a federally assisted meal program for underprivileged students. I was too embarrassed to eat my free lunch every day, as it was a clear and obvious sign that I did not fit in. More often than not, I skipped collecting my free lunch and instead ate whatever food my friends shared with me, or I went hungry.

Knowing my classmates had far superior opportunities and resources didn't stop me from comparing myself to my peers. It was a damaging viewpoint. Comparing myself to others was an exercise in pain and futility. I didn't have the opportunities and advantages that they had, and nothing would change that imbalance. The only way I was going to create something better for my life, with my life, was to focus on what I could do, not what I couldn't do. To focus on what I was, not on what I wasn't. I needed to set aside this impossible standard of comparison.

> The only way I was going to create something better for my life...was to focus on what I could do, not what I couldn't do.

The best way to make the most of myself was to focus on myself. To be responsible to and for myself, first and foremost. To truly mind my own business. Comparing myself to others, even to my idea of what I could be, was perhaps human nature, but comparison robbed me of confidence, acknowledgement of my accomplishments, and my worth. Comparison created false beliefs and faulty expectations between my current success and my future success.

After high school, I continued to compare myself to classmates I'd known years before. I continued to believe I was a have-not, and while I could become more successful in my life, I believed I would never be one of the haves. Because I was so focused on comparing myself to the haves, I didn't allow myself to have "too much" until after I stopped comparing myself to others.

Despite my awareness of comparison being a bad habit, I still catch myself comparing from time to time. That's okay, I'm not perfect. But now I see that habit as a signal to redirect my attention from someone else to me.

I take the opportunity to recognize my awesome skills and abilities, and the unique contribution I give to the world. I use the comparison to learn from other people's successes and mistakes. I find ways to motivate myself to make progress on my goals. I focus on what's in front of me.

This redirection is easier said than done, of course, but having a toolbox of strategies to help you change your focus from comparing yourself to others to focusing on yourself can make the process easier.

Mind Your Own Business

Catching yourself in the act of comparison is a good first step. Notice when you are focused on what someone else is doing—whether positive or negative. Are you down on yourself when a peer receives an award? Are you annoyed with your coworker's late arrival the third time this week? Thinking or talking about what someone else is doing is one way you compare yourself to others and stop focusing on the badass that is you!

What else could you do when you catch yourself in the comparison act? Redirect your attention to yourself any time you notice your thoughts or words lingering on someone else. Instead of judging yourself for this habit, stop and ask yourself, "What is one thing I can do right now to improve my situation?" Now go do that one thing.

Every time you redirect your attention to yourself and what you can do, it gets a little easier. With time you'll notice you spend less time paying attention to others.

Acknowledge Your Choices

When you compare yourself to others, you often conveniently overlook the choices and hard work they have made to get where they are today. You may not be willing to make the sacrifices they made, or endure the hardships they faced to reach their goals. You probably won't ever know how hard they had it and what choices they made, especially when it seems they had it easy.

Be happy with your choices and, if you're not, know that you have the opportunity to make different choices at any time on any day. Focus on living a life that works for you and achieve success at your own pace.

Be Where You Are

You won't be as successful as someone with years of experience when you're just getting started. Jon Acuff says, "Never compare your beginning to somebody else's middle."

Stop expecting yourself to be further along in the process. It's okay to be a beginner. Enjoy where you are as you work toward your goals.

There will always be someone who started before you and someone who started after you. Your greatest power and ability to make progress comes from being where you are.

Learn from Someone Else's Experience

Instead of comparing yourself to what other people have accomplished, why not benefit from it? You have the option to jump-start your success by learning from someone else's experience. Ask a more successful person to be your coach or mentor. If they are unable to work with you long term, they may be willing to answer a few questions about what they've learned. Look for the opportunity to develop a valuable contact, and maybe even a friend.

Make Progress on Your Goals

When you compare yourself to others, you distract yourself from your goals. When you redirect your attention, time, and efforts to your purpose, you make progress on your goals and stop worrying about what everyone else is doing.

Be Unique

You have your own voice, your own experience, and your own talents that no one else has! Your gift to the world comes through sharing your unique perspective, not copying someone else's. When you compare yourself to others, you minimize what's great about you. Making your own mark on the world builds confidence in yourself and lasting success.

Celebrate Your Success

Jon Acuff reminds us that "Other people's success is not an indication of your failure." Instead of reacting negatively to a comparison, remember this: Today you are right where you need to be. Enjoy the peace that comes with patience and allow yourself to keep pace with your success.

When you start comparing yourself to others, think of ways to leverage your experience to motivate and grow yourself. It's important to focus on what you can change, and what you can change is you.

How to Say No

As a recovering people-pleaser and a serial volunteer, I say yes a lot. I'm so eager to prove my worth, to make something of myself, I don't always think about the consequences before agreeing to help. The people-pleasing voice in my head constantly asks, "If you're not providing value in this world, what are you doing with your life?"

Luckily, I've cultivated some responses to help quiet that voice:

- I'm living my true purpose.
- I'm enjoying my life.
- I deserve to be happy, and the only person I can make happy is me.
- Disappointing the right people means not disappointing myself.
- I can't choose who I disappoint if I never say no.

Unless you've got tons of extra time on hand, endless resources, and the patience of a saint, you're going to need to say no sometimes. Let me put it this way—every time you say yes to one thing, you say no to something else. No to a different opportunity, no to free time, or no to family, close friends, and, well, yourself. Think about how often you put off the things you want for yourself. What have you been telling yourself you'll finally do *for you* after things slow down at work, or after the kids are back in school, or after the holidays are over? You're saying no to yourself so you can say yes to everything else.

> Let me put it this way—every time you say yes to one thing, you say no to something else.

Think about a time you wanted to say no and didn't. Maybe you agreed to take on a project you didn't have the time or expertise to handle. Chances are you either didn't do a good job on the project, worked yourself into exhaustion, or let something else slide to get the work done properly. How did that make you feel? Overwhelmed? Resentful? Frustrated? My guess is it didn't feel good.

Saying no is a great way to increase your capabilities, your competence, and your confidence! When someone can trust you to say yes only when you really mean it—when you have the time and experience to excel at the task—they begin to trust you more overall, and they also begin to respect when you say no. They learn that when you say no, it means you can't perform in the same way as when you say yes. When you say no, you even begin to trust yourself more.

Saying no isn't always easy. Fortunately I have a simple tip for knowing when to say no: Say no when you are unwilling or unable to agree. See, I told you it was simple!

Before you throw the book across the room, let me explain what it looks like to be unwilling or unable to say yes.

What Does Unwilling to Say Yes Look Like?

Maybe a friend wants to set you up on a blind date, and you'd rather sit at home alone and binge Netflix. Maybe your boss wants you to stay late and you'd rather sit at home alone and binge Netflix. Maybe you've been invited to a friend of a friend's baby shower and you're just not that into babies you aren't personally related to and you'd rather sit at home alone and binge Netflix. (My introversion may be showing, and I'd rather sit at home alone and binge Netflix.)

If you are unwilling, it means you don't want to. Please, stop doing things you don't want to do! Stop doing things to make someone else happy, to be polite, or because you think you "should" do it. If you're a people-pleaser like me, this might be incredibly difficult. You might be so used to being focused on what other people want, you don't even know what you want. To keep your wants in mind as you make decisions, keep asking the question, "What do

I want?" Eventually you'll start to get a better sense of all your wants.

Saying no is easier said than done, but I promise you, other people will be more open to it than you think. When I was twenty-one years old, I was working at a local sporting goods company. The CEO of the company asked me to stay late to prepare a financial report for him. That particular night I wasn't willing to stay late. The day had been especially challenging and all I wanted to do was go home and relax. Because I was unwilling to work late, I said no. Instead of working late, I asked if I could come in early the next day and get the report to him first thing in the morning. He agreed.

He wasn't mad. I didn't get fired. The world did not end. I said no and everything was okay—better than okay!

In addition to being unwilling, I was not at my best after a difficult day, and I knew I'd do better work in the morning. It was better for both of us that I said no and postponed my yes. What would have happened if I had stayed late and made an error due to my exhaustion? It could have been worse than mustering the courage to say no to my boss.

What Does Unable to Say Yes Look Like?

Being unable to say yes usually happens when you lack the resources to follow through on what you're being asked to do. Your resources include skills and experience, time, energy, desire, and money. It doesn't matter if you think you "should" do what you're being asked. If you are unable to do it, you need to say no.

Think about all the times you are solicited for a charitable cause. They may all be good causes, but that doesn't mean you can afford to give money to them all. You'd go broke! Or what if a friend invites you to a dinner you really can't afford, but you don't want to say no, so you go anyway, and then you're short on your rent or other bills. Wouldn't you have been better off saying no in the first place?

And while we're on the subject of being unable to say yes, give yourself permission to say no when a request or opportunity is not aligned with the life you want. If the local veterinary association recognizes that you did an excellent job rehabilitating your rescue cat and invites you to speak but you're not pursuing a career as the cat whisperer, you might want to decline the invitation. There are plenty of worthy, exciting, and even great opportunities out there that will distract you from the badass life you are creating. The more distracted you get and the more time you spend doing things that don't further your goals, the longer it will take to reach your goal.

> **There are plenty of... opportunities out there that will distract you from the badass life you are creating.**

Now you have some idea of when to say no, but how to do it is another challenge.

"No" is a complete sentence. "No" is all you have to say. In fact, I strongly encourage you to not justify your no. You don't need a defensible reason to say no. Your reason doesn't have to be good enough for anyone but you. The more you make excuses for saying no, the more you support the belief that saying no isn't okay unless you have a really, really, really good reason. Or a really, really, really good white lie. Just say, "No."

You might be afraid of sounding rude, but there are polite ways to say no without including an excuse. For example, "Thank you for thinking of me, but I cannot commit to that project right now." Or, "I appreciate the invitation; however, I won't make it. Please invite me again in the future." You may also reply, "Are there other ways I can contribute?" By saying no, you can change yourself from a people-pleaser into a person-pleaser, wherein you please yourself. If you can't please anyone but yourself, make sure you're pleasing at least that one person.

Get Fired Up

It's shocking to look back and realize how often I've gone along with something I didn't want because I felt pressured or obligated, or was simply unable to consider my own wants and needs first. Failing to consider my wants and needs is a social behavior I grew up with, and one I know many other women did as well.

The #MeToo movement started with women collectively speaking out about sexual assault. On the heels of #MeToo, a woman named Grace told the story of her unwanted and distressing sexual encounter with celebrity Aziz Ansari on Babe.net, a lifestyle site for young women. Grace went on a date with Ansari and was unable to speak up as their encounter became more and more uncomfortable, eventually escalating to sexual acts she didn't want to engage in but was unable to stop.

When the story broke, social media blew up with strong reactions from all sides. Grace's story was all too familiar and personally relatable. I recognized how many times I, like Grace, was unable to clearly set a boundary and express my needs, or even consider my health, well-being, and safety on a date. Based on her account, Grace, like myself and many women I know, found herself in an undesirable situation, unable to fully recognize and express her discomfort because of years of social conditioning that taught her to defer to the needs of others before her own.

After reading Grace's story, I had conversations with both men and women about the difficulty of recognizing my needs and speaking up for myself in one-on-one relationships in particular. I had an ah-ha moment when I realized this behavior didn't only show up for me in intimate or romantic partnerships. It is often easier to observe in intimate settings, especially now that society has started discussing the problem, but once I was aware of the pattern, I realized I had experienced it plenty of times in professional relationships, too.

Here's an example of what that dynamic looks like in a professional relationship: I hired a business consultant to help me grow my business. Unfortunately, the partnership just wasn't working for me. I knew my needs were not being met, but I struggled to recognize what I needed and, once I did, I found it difficult to speak up and ask for what I needed.

I had paid for unlimited access to my consultant's guidance and expertise, and on average waited three to five days for a response to time-sensitive emails. At her suggestion, I tagged her repeatedly in questions posted in an online forum and often did not receive a response. When we did connect, something felt off. I felt anxious before our meetings and discouraged after.

Like Grace, I made feeble attempts to express my wants and needs, not being direct enough to get my needs met. I sent emails to my business consultant explaining the partnership was not what I expected, rather than stating outright that I wasn't happy and wasn't getting what I needed. I asked, "How can I get the most value out of our relationship," trying to find out what I could do differently—assuming my actions could change the fact that she wasn't responding to my emails. I felt like a huge pain in the ass as I tried to communicate my needs, as if asking for what I wanted was a disruption to someone I was paying handsomely to advise me.

My attempts to ask for what I wanted became progressively stronger and clearer, and the business relationship still did not improve. I began to lose trust in her, as well as myself. I did not feel she was on my side, nor earning the money I was paying her, and yet it was still difficult to express my needs. I worried about inconveniencing my business consultant by asking for something different than the level of service she was providing. A few people close to me noticed something was bothering me. I asked a few friends and colleagues for ideas on how I could communicate my needs better.

"Maybe I just need to suck it up and make the best of it," I said to a friend.

"You're paying a lot of money for a service you're not happy with," she replied. "That's not okay. You deserve better."

Her words stuck with me. It was not okay. I was not okay in this relationship. I recognized my familiar behavior of considering the needs of other people before considering what was best for me. I realized I was repeating a pattern and was once again taking care of myself only after everyone else was taken care of. In this case, I was more concerned with my consultant's feelings than my own. I deserved better.

> I realized I...was once again taking care of myself only after everyone else was taken care of.

I was stressed and unhappy until I ended the relationship, firing the business consultant I had hired a few months earlier. When Grace's story posted, I realized how much I related to Grace, not only in past unwanted sexual encounters, but also in my partnership with this former business consultant. When I left that relationship—like Grace—I left in tears. Firing that consultant was, like my divorce and bankruptcy, one of the hardest and one of the best decisions I ever made.

My awareness of this behavioral pattern—of women giving in to pressure from other people to meet their needs—has been growing since I fired that consultant. After my ah-ha moment and reading other #MeToo stories, more and more I realized how pervasive this social construct is among women. This pattern shows up in your personal and professional life. It happens when you're on a date and engage in any sexual act you aren't really into. It happens at work when your boss makes unreasonable requests and you feel obligated to give in. It happens when you give your clients whatever they demand at the cost of your own best interests. In what other situations does it show up for you?

> Remember: You don't owe anyone anything.
>
> Don't give anything unless you give it willingly.
>
> Your wants and needs are just as important as anyone else's.
>
> You deserve better.

Women are taught to be accommodating and pleasant, to be nice and quiet and unassuming. Women are taught they should be mothers and caregivers. Since the rise of the self-help industry, the world started to consider ideas like codependency, self-care, and the female orgasm. Women's interests and needs became more openly discussed, and as a woman, I felt somewhat liberated.

And yet, all too often, women still fail to consider their own best interests. Oh, women are allowed to put themselves first in a case of life-threatening emergency (such as when an airplane oxygen mask is needed), or when facing a serious illness. They're also free to consider their best interests when everything is alright, aka, when everyone else is taken care of. When the kids are off at college, or your partner has a stable, important position at work, only *then* are you free to consider yourself. But in everyday situations, when faced with the wants and needs of others at work and home, women are expected to put their needs last, to the point that many of us don't even know what we want.

In the classic what's-for-dinner scenario, the woman just can't make up her mind. But the problem isn't that she is indecisive—the problem is she probably doesn't know what she wants! And even when she does know, she's so used to going along with what other people want that expressing her own opinion feels wild and reckless.

To break yourself of this pattern and figure out what you want, ask yourself, "What outcome will benefit me?" This question will sound bold at first, it may feel selfish and unreasonable, and you may cringe at the thought of it. Who do you think you are?! A Bridezilla? (The idea of a woman with strong opinions is literally comparable to a monster, think on that.) But considering your best interests is different than acting on them. It's not the same as suggesting your best interests should come at the expense of others. Asking this question normalizes the experience of knowing what you want. It normalizes the experience of questioning what outcome is best for you. Later, you can decide if acting in your best interests makes sense and if it's something you want to do.

Keep in mind, acting in your best interests doesn't have to mean doing so at the expense of others. There are many situations when acting in your best interests will have no effect, or have a neutral effect, on others. And sometimes, acting in your best interests, when it's the right thing to do, may have a negative effect on one person and simultaneously have a positive effect on many others.

You are gifted. You are talented. The world needs your talents and gifts. The best way to share your gifts and talents with the world is to consider your best interests from time to time. Or, you know, all the time! Prioritizing your interests puts you in a position to do more badass stuff—the stuff the world is waiting for.

Be Awesomely Selfish

I'm going to tell you something that goes against everything you were taught watching *Sesame Street:* to be successful in life you need to be selfish.

This selfishness doesn't need to come at the expense of others, but maybe at the expense of politeness. Sometimes at the expense of niceness. Sometimes at the expense of putting other people's hopes and dreams before your own because you have BIG DREAMS! You have big goals and big plans and you're going to achieve them. To do so, you need to spend time, money, and energy pursuing those BIG DREAMS, which means, you need to be more selfish.

> **You need to spend time, money, and energy pursuing those BIG DREAMS.... You need to be more selfish.**

When I started my business, I needed to be a lot more selfish. That included saying no to social invitations that were a drain on my time and energy, so I could redirect those resources into building my business. I met a lot of people while I was networking and received a lot of invitations for coffee. Some of these requests came from people who were aligned with my business values and goals. Other requests came from perfectly pleasant and interesting people who were not aligned with my business values and goals, including people who primarily saw me as a potential client. While they had their own (selfish) interests at heart, I wasn't going to reach my goals by accepting every coffee invitation. In the growth stage of my business, I chose to be selfish and prioritize my goals and my time.

Now you may be reading this and thinking, "Prioritizing goals doesn't actually sound that selfish—it sounds smart. What successful business owner doesn't prioritize goals?" While it doesn't *sound* selfish, in practice it often *feels* selfish.

As a recovering people-pleaser, it was challenging to decline coffee dates and requests for business meetings without a clear agenda. Setting boundaries around my time may not have appeared selfish to others, but it felt selfish to me. I felt conceited, thinking I was "so important" that I could turn down invitations, and thinking that I was going to be "so successful" that I could put my goals before others. Making my business a priority conflicted with my people-pleasing ways, even if my actions didn't look outwardly selfish. It took many reminders that I am important and that my business is successful before I really believed that setting boundaries and putting my goals first were necessary selfishness.

In the first three years of my business, I invested money into the business and wasn't making a big profit. Our finances were stretched to the max and I felt so selfish about how I was spending our money. My partner missed out on concerts and events he wanted to attend. He made do with with his old desktop computer that would freeze and reboot in the middle of a task. Being selfish with my money also meant I didn't buy many gifts on birthdays and holidays, even when friends and family bought nice gifts for me. In those first few years of my business, I saved my money for me, to invest in me.

Prioritizing my business financially not only felt selfish to me, it may have appeared selfish to others, too. I thought of the times growing up I heard a family member sneer when someone spent money on themselves. I imagined my family had similar remarks to make about my current choices. Still, none of my friends or family complained. Maybe they were just being polite. Maybe being selfish after so many years of selfless giving didn't seem so unreasonable to those close to me. Maybe they loved and supported me enough to watch me succeed, and that was more important than gifts and convenience. Just because I felt selfish didn't mean everyone saw me as being selfish, and even if they did, it didn't mean it was wrong to do.

Putting yourself first isn't really a new idea in this book. During the safety demonstration on an airplane, we are advised to put on our own oxygen mask in an emergency before assisting others. Remember, society allows us to put ourselves first in an emergency scenario. But you can't achieve your BIG DREAMS if you only think about yourself during an emergency! Stop waiting until you're suffering from chronic illness. Stop waiting until your toxic job has you crying in your car at lunch. Stop waiting for something to go wrong to give yourself permission to be selfish. What if, instead, you were more selfish right now, and then you used your success to help others?

> **It's about time you started putting yourself first.**

For years, I looked after my interests only after everyone else was taken care of. I devoted enough energy and time to myself so that my work and determination got me out of poverty. I survived abuse and mental illness and was okay. But at some point I decided just surviving wasn't enough. I wanted more. I wanted to thrive. I wanted to make a difference, to positively impact the world, and that took a new level of selfishness. I started filling my lungs with oxygen each and every day, breathing deep and taking my fill. I started to thrive.

It's about time you started putting yourself first. You need to be more selfish to succeed. Practice being okay with *feeling* selfish, because that's really the trick of it, isn't it? You can rationalize an idea in your mind and recognize the logic behind that idea, but it's an entirely different experience to face your feelings and fears and put that idea into practice.

Like all the ideas in this book, it starts with you—believing in you, doing for you, and taking that scary and uncomfortable first step to improve your circumstances. Go ahead, be selfish.

Be Demanding

As you begin to feel more comfortable with being selfish (go you!), take it a step further and think about being demanding.

When I think of people who are demanding, I think of people I don't like. I think of people who use and abuse others for their own personal gain. But demands don't have to come at the expense of others. Demanding people don't have to be mean or ugly. Demands are what come after considering your best interests. Demands are forcefully asking for something you want or need.

You need to demand what's necessary for you to create boundaries supporting your personal safety, growth, and expansion. This includes unapologetically sharing your thoughts and feelings, saying no, expressing your needs, and speaking up for yourself. It's okay to demand something even if it's not what someone else wants; these demands are about *your* best interests.

- Ask for more money.
- Tell your boss you won't work late.
- Take credit for your work instead of letting credit go to someone else or to the whole team.
- Express disappointment.
- Speak loud and clear.
- Be direct and specific.

Demands can be difficult to make when you're not used to asking for what you want. Up your asking game by asking for what you want more often. These are not meek requests; they are *demands* for what you need. Don't allow other people's interests and concerns to be more important than your own. If you encounter someone who thrives on taking advantage of others, well, no doubt this person will cry foul at your attempt to be demanding, but please recognize this jackass for what they are. They don't have your best interests at heart. Are you noticing the theme? Put yourself first. Consider your best interests. Be selfish. Be demanding.

> Chances are your attempts to be demanding will actually be reasonable requests similar to the requests other people frequently make.

Here's what I expect will happen if you go out in the world with the intention of being demanding: I expect you will do or say something that feels and sounds bold to you, but that other people will think is perfectly normal and reasonable. If you're like me, chances are your attempts to be demanding will actually be reasonable requests similar to the requests other people frequently make. It won't even sound that demanding. But to you it can feel like a BIG DEAL if you aren't used to putting yourself first.

Let's consider a small, easy opportunity for you to ask for what you want. Say you go out to dinner with your BFF and the hostess leads you to a table and asks, "Will this be okay?" You'd really rather sit in the corner booth, away from the drafty door. Normally you might mumble, "Yes, thank you," but today you muster up your courage and say, "I'd like the corner booth—is that available?"

In my experiments with being demanding, the hostess will typically show you to the corner booth without a fuss because the hostess is used to other people making these types of requests. While I haven't had it happen yet, I suppose the hostess might reply, "No, I'm sorry that booth isn't available." No harm, no foul, am I right?

But wait. You don't have to stop there. If your first preference isn't available, what if you asked for your next preference—a table away from the drafty door? Chances are good that even if it's not your first pick, you'll be seated at a more desirable table.

Sticking with the restaurant theme, let's say you've asked twice for a water refill and you're still sitting at the table with an empty glass. What if you—gulp—flagged down a waiter—any waiter—and said, "I would like more water. Can you get that for me?"

These low-risk requests were once difficult for me. I avoided speaking up because I didn't want to create extra work for anyone. As much as possible, I avoided disturbing anyone or anything. I moved through my life making as little impact as possible. I assumed my needs were less important than those of the people around me, even when I was paying for a service. This pattern of staying silent was present throughout my life, from restaurant service to my relationships at work. But I couldn't succeed by continuing this meek behavior. The challenges of poverty, domestic violence, sexual assault, and mental illness meant I had to demand accommodations and opportunities in a world that wasn't designed to allow people in my circumstances to succeed. To practice making demands, I started by making small requests and, as I got more comfortable, I got better at making bigger requests, then making demands when appropriate.

I'm still working on it and I want you to join me. I want you to be more demanding—a lot more demanding. Start with small stuff like asking for exactly what you want at a restaurant, and work up to bigger stuff like asking for a raise, dumping the friend who drains you, or going after what you really want in life, even when you're scared shitless to do it. Get comfortable with the feeling of being demanding. Let your voice be heard. Create a disruption. Leave an impression. Take up your space in the world. Don't wait for someone else to give you a chance—demand it.

High School Hell

The high school I attended was a "HIGH" achieving school as rated by the state Department of Education. With a rich tradition of academic and athletic excellence, boasting famous alumni including a Broadway star, NBA and NFL athletes, and the founder of a major software company, my family didn't quite fit the culture the school administrators wanted to promote. My mom was a single parent with a mental illness and my family was poor.

A few weeks into my older sister's freshman year, the principal called my sister into his office. She had rarely excelled academically, but her artistic talents were well above average. With effort, she might have been able to find a place for herself at the high school, but she lacked the motivation or desire to fit in where she was not welcomed.

And the principal made it clear she was not welcome.

With frank cruelty he told her, "Look, we both know you're going to drop out eventually, so why don't you do everyone here a favor and drop out now? You're wasting school resources that could go to the students who want to be here."

Believing what he said was true, my sister dropped out of high school. She either didn't care or didn't have it in her to try and prove him wrong. When no one believes in you, it's much harder to believe in yourself.

The following year I started as a freshman at the same school. I knew what that horrible principal had said to my sister and wondered what he'd say to me. I struggled with depression, anxiety, and PTSD, but I'd always been the high achiever of the family.

The principal never singled me out like he did my sister. Maybe I was marginally more acceptable than she was. Maybe my academic achievements gave me an edge. Maybe my hard work that allowed me to maintain a B average while taking Advanced Placement classes, participating in choir and theater, and juggling my own mental health and an unstable home environment kept me on a scale that he deemed passable.

But I was always waiting for him to tell me I wasn't worthy, and I struggled more and more to maintain my place in school as my life continued to be defined by the circumstances that set me apart from my high school peers.

My mom, a licensed practical nurse, picked up shifts at local hospitals and health care facilities. While moving a bedridden patient, she suffered an injury that ended her nursing career—or any other career. My absentee father had stopped paying child support again, my stepfather was long gone, and we barely got by on welfare. My mom spent months in physical therapy in debilitating pain. One day after an excruciatingly painful physical therapy appointment, she attempted suicide. I came home from school to the news that my mom was in the psychiatric hospital.

The physical stress of her injury worsened her mental health, putting her in and out of the psychiatric hospital. I was sixteen when my mom was diagnosed with dissociative identity disorder, at the time known as multiple personality disorder. She had lived with her mental illness most of her life until the intense pain of her back injury caused her to have a breakdown. The first suicide attempt wouldn't be her last.

Workers' comp finally agreed to additional testing, and MRI results revealed her injury would require complicated and painful back surgery. After multiple back surgeries, my mom was barely able to take care of herself, let alone her three daughters.

As "the responsible one," I was added as a signer on my mom's checking account. Whenever she was unable, I paid the rent and household bills, bought groceries, and with the help of my older sister, got my eight-year-old sister to and from school every day. I only screwed up once, overdrawing the bank account by a few hundred dollars.

Somehow I took primary responsibility for the household and mostly kept up with my classes. I did most of my homework at school, during lunch or on a free period. I rarely paid attention to the teacher in math class, preferring to use class time to complete my homework.

Neither my older sister nor I had a car or driver's license, making grocery shopping or running other errands difficult. I took the bus or walked three-quarters of a mile to the grocery store each week. I relied on rides from friends to get to and from school and for other errands. I diligently deposited any social services checks that came from the state, walking a half-mile to the bank and back.

I came directly home from school most days, starting dinner while I packed my sister's lunch for the next day. I washed up after dinner, completed any remaining homework, and put my younger sister to bed before crawling into my own bed. I stayed up late to read, escaping into science fiction, fantasy, and horror stories. It was the only time I had to myself and it was my only escape.

While workers' comp delayed my mom's injury claim, our family scraped by on disability and welfare. We scarcely had enough money to buy groceries, forget about any incidentals. We were evicted from the duplex we rented and my older sister moved in with a friend. My mom, my younger sister, and I moved to a smaller apartment across town, leaving behind some of our belongings in our rushed relocation.

After four years, I graduated high school without my diploma. While I met all the technical requirements for graduation, my high school would not give me my diploma due to less than $80 in unpaid school fees—fees my family still could not pay.

The day of my high school graduation was a sunny, warm Saturday in May. In a shiny marigold polyester cap and gown, I walked in the commencement ceremony. In an empty gesture, they called my name and handed me the empty certificate holder.

I stood there, sun shining in my eyes, the marigold yellow of my gown at odds with my skin tone. I plastered a smile on my face as my aunt, my mom, and my younger sister cheered me on from the bleachers. That day I understood I didn't have the same opportunities as those around me; I felt it to my very core. The system was not created to support or encourage me to succeed. If I was going to succeed, I had to do it my way, on my terms. I didn't know how to create something better for myself, but I was determined to find a way.

Progress, Not Perfection

My perfectionism served a purpose in helping me rise above my circumstances, and it harmed me deeply. Perfectionism pushed me to keep going when I had every reason to give up. Perfectionism also told me I was not enough. I was never enough. I was no good. I was awful. I was shit. Like the little girl who threw her school paper in the trash, I believed I was bad.

But that's bullshit. That's the head trash talking. I am not, nor have I ever been, no good, awful, bad, or shit. I am enough. I'll say it again, I am enough. So are you. You are enough. You are more than enough. Maybe you believe you will be enough when you finally achieve whatever your fill-in-the-blank goal is. NOPE. You're enough now. Stop valuing yourself on what you aren't yet and start valuing yourself on what you are. You are good, wonderful, amazing, beautiful.

In this journey of life, there is no perfect—there is only progress. Many of us have that cruel inner voice that keeps moving the finish line. As soon as you achieve one goal, it's already pointing you to the next destination, telling you how much farther you have to go. Or, worse yet, when you haven't even reached your initial goal, that voice changes the goal, so it feels like you never accomplish anything. But focusing on progress rather than end-goal achievements helps stop that voice and helps you value what you are now.

Stopping to acknowledge your progress helps you build on what you've accomplished. It allows you to integrate the growth and experience you've gained to create a better life. Your life is improved through the journey to reach your goal rather than achievement of the goal itself. With every step along the way, you grow your skills, expand your experience, and step into becoming who you are meant to be. Focusing on progress makes it easier to celebrate your accomplishments and little victories so you can build confidence in yourself, and so you can learn to believe in yourself. Celebrating your progress allows you to *be* in your journey, giving you the opportunity to fully experience and enjoy your life while you're living it. What's the point of creating a better life if you don't enjoy it? Perfectionism and focusing on achieving the next goal, and the next goal, and the next goal creates more effort and challenge. Haven't you had enough of that already?

In my twenties, I began studying yoga after stumbling upon the cable yoga program *Yoga Zone*. What I learned about the practice of yoga pierced the armor of my perfectionism. The yoga itself was pretty great—breathing, stretching, and being fully present in my body was a powerful exercise—but the application of the principles, or sutras, of yoga had a greater influence on my health and wellness. They became something I could apply to my life, a reminder that effort is more important than results. I was so inspired by the sutras, I tattooed the yoga sutras "abhyasa" and "vairagya" on my outer thigh as a daily reminder to be present in my yoga practice and in my life.

Abhyasa and vairagya are translated from sanskrit as *practice* and *dispassion*. When related to yoga, abhyasa and vairagya are practiced as purposeful action without judgement of the outcome. I apply myself, doing the work, without worry or concern about how far I get or what I achieve in yoga or in life. I am unattached to judgment. I let go. This discipline is perfectionism kryptonite. When the outcome is irrelevant, the work itself is what matters. Practice makes progress.

The first step to focusing on progress begins with nurturing the seed of self-worth as discussed in Chapter 9: The Seed of Self-Worth. You start with one action—shifting a belief, trying a different approach, responding instead of reacting, or practicing any of the other tools in this book. Take action, and then acknowledge your progress as you work toward change instead of waiting to give yourself credit until after you achieve a goal. Celebrate your progress by telling a friend, accountability partner, or mentor what you've been up to. Recognize your progress on your gratitude list. Look for any opportunity to be proud of your progress. You can't fail because it's not about doing it right, it's just about doing it.

If you get overwhelmed, take a break. Intentional breaks count as progress because they are about being aware of yourself and your limits while practicing radical self-love and unconditional self-care. After your break, start again by using a tool that's worked for you in the past. Take it a step at a time—which step is not as important as the fact that you consistently take steps. With each step, acknowledge your progress. Even if it doesn't *feel like* you're making progress—you are!

If your face is scrunched up with doubt right about now (go ahead, check yo' face), here's another way to think about progress, not perfection: Do your best and forget the rest.

Building Confidence

Confidence allows me to take risks, to make bold choices, and to follow my dreams. Confidence is believing I'll be successful before I get started. To improve my situation, to be wildly successful creating the life I want, confidence is required. That doesn't mean I don't experience self-doubt. Actually, I still experience it regularly. It would be nice to have more self-confidence before I go out and do big, bold things, but it takes going out and doing big, bold things to build confidence.

Writing this book took confidence I didn't yet have. I traveled 3,300 miles to attend a writing retreat in Hawaii and, full of confidence, my first attempt was a complete and total failure! It was a significant setback to my plans, and I came home not knowing how to write the book I knew I wanted to write. About six months later, I took what I had learned from that first attempt and in the months between and wrote the first draft of what would become this book. My confidence level had grown because of the first risk I took.

Confidence comes from stepping outside my comfort zone. Confidence comes from falling flat on my face... and picking myself up again. It comes from learning from those face-plants, gaining the experience of failure, and knowing how to do things differently next time. Think about a child learning to walk—they become more confident, and more capable, as they try and fall and try again. They aren't afraid to start. They aren't afraid to fall. They keep trying until they get it.

When I made the decision at eight years old to create a better life for myself, I didn't know how to do it. I decided that I would have a better life and, like a small child learning to walk, I kept trying until I got it. Or, I kept trying until things got better because, honestly, I'm still trying. The more I try, the better and better life gets, and the more confident I feel.

Writing this book wasn't the first time I fell flat on my face. In my senior year of high school I fell hard. A few months into the school year, a close friend of mine died under questionable circumstances. The shock and confusion around her death left me reeling. My grades crashed as a result. It would have been all too easy for me to fall apart, to give up, to drop out like my older sister had a few years earlier, but I was determined to turn things around. I showed up every day and tried my best. There were days when it was difficult to put in that work. Some days my best was better than others. Eventually I succeeded in turning my grades around and getting back on track. My chemistry teacher nicknamed me "Renaissance Woman" for my noteworthy improvement. Rebuilding my grades and academic reputation was a lot of hard work that helped build my confidence and became a source of confidence when I faced other challenges.

As an adult, there have been more situations when it was hard to put myself out there and not give up after a setback. Sometimes I need a little encouragement to get going, and you may need some too. If you're not feeling particularly confident at the moment, try this exercise:

Make a list of everything you like about yourself and everything you're good at. Let's call it your What I Like About Me list. If this is difficult for you, ask a friend or family member to help you. (Make sure you ask someone you know has your back, not that "helpful" person who means well but will point out all your faults, or will tell you one good thing for every two bad things.)

Keep adding to your list every day. Nothing is too small to go on the list. Do you like the way your lip curls when you smile? On the list! Do you love your ability to laugh at puns? On the list! Do you appreciate your badass Excel skills? On the list! Your What I Like About Me list might even overlap with your gratitude list. (Because you're keeping that list, too, aren't you?) Be actively grateful for you! Because you? You're brilliant. You're fucking amazing. And you're most definitely enough.

In fact, let me just say, I'm grateful for you. Thank you for buying and reading my book. For reals, yo. You're on my gratitude list!

Use your What I Like About Me list and your gratitude list to encourage and motivate yourself as you get started doing big, bold things. And hey, if that "I love you" mirror practice in Chapter 7: Radical Self-Love wasn't awkward enough for you, look at yourself in the mirror and read your lists out loud to yourself. Boo-ya! You'll build confidence in no time!

> **You're a badass for doing the work, regardless of the results.**

As you keep working to develop your confidence, recognize your progress and appreciate how far you've come. You're a badass for doing the work, regardless of the results. Keep stretching, keep appreciating, keep progressing. Go make magic, you beautiful badass.

Is Life Hard or Easy?

I've had a particularly hard life. I grew up in poverty and experienced trauma at an early age. Through my teenage years I had to grow up fast and take care of my younger sister and my ailing mother. I was divorced and filed for bankruptcy before I was thirty. I had to fight and work hard for everything I have. My life story has taught me life is hard. But what if life can be easy?

As a lifelong bootstrapper I tend to approach challenges with great effort and determination. I believe life is hard, and so it is. It's not just my belief that makes life hard, though. Sometimes life is genuinely hard. Sometimes the odds are stacked against me. Sometimes I've got to put on my big girl underwear, knuckle down, and do some hard stuff.

The thing is, I've discovered that approaching every situation with that same get-it-done, grr argh point of view makes my experience harder! If I believe life is hard, I gather my strength and my courage and tackle problems head-on. While this is effective, and certainly does accomplish *something*, this approach can lead to overlooking simpler and easier solutions, including asking for help, clarifying expectations, or negotiating terms. I choose to stop believing work and life are hard, and start believing in an easier path.

Years ago when I started blogging about work-life balance, I was on the edge of burnout. I worked so hard at everything I did that my health and happiness suffered. I underwent seven surgeries in six years, each surgery with varying levels of complications. When I was thirty-five, I experienced a painful bout of shingles—a disease my doctor assured me was brought on by stress. I hadn't taken a vacation for years, using my money and my paid time off for medical procedures, doctors appointments, and physical therapy. Believing life was hard was hard on my body.

The high levels of self-inflicted stress threatened to sabotage the progress and success I had created for myself. I started to recognize this pattern the next time I faced a challenge at work and once again prepared to bootstrap my efforts to deal with the situation.

My coworker was planning a three-week vacation during our busiest season. I didn't know how I would manage to do my work and cover for her, but I would find a way. My old way of thinking affirmed that life was hard, and this challenge was the proof. I prepared myself to work 60+ hours for three weeks to meet our seasonal deadlines, complete my work, and complete hers, too.

While I was preparing for a month of long hours and exhaustion, I hit my breaking point. Finally, I'd had

Is Life Hard or Easy?

enough. What if this situation wasn't as hard as I made it out to be? What if there was another way to deal with my coworker's absence? The last thing I wanted was another major health crisis. I decided to find another solution. I chose to stop making everything so fucking hard.

In my new enlightened state of mind, I started by brainstorming my options. I made a list of all the possible ways I could handle the situation, from the unreasonable (run away to a foreign country with twenty-five bucks and a cracker, work myself to an early grave, quit my job and live off the money I get from robbing a bank) to some more reasonable, easier options (say no, ask for help, set boundaries).

As I wrote out my options from the absurd to the astute, a smile sprung to my lips and I began to laugh. Oh my, how difficult I made life out to be! In that moment I knew exactly what to do.

I drafted an email to my bosses, informing them I would be unable to do all the work and meet all the deadlines to cover for my coworker's vacation. I proposed two solutions:

> Let me know which option you prefer, and I'll take care of the details!

Option 1: Miss our filing deadlines and pay associated fines and penalties, estimated between $3,000–$4,000.

Option 2: Hire a temp to cover the staff shortage, estimated between $4,000–$6,000.

I would prefer to hire a temp and meet our filing deadlines but I understand the cost is significantly higher and I will work with whatever option you choose.

Which option did my bosses choose? They chose secret option number three! They informed my coworker her three-week vacation was not approved during our busiest time of the year, and asked her to move her trip a few weeks earlier or later.

> I can choose the easy way!

Ah, so life is not so hard after all. It was my approach that made it harder than it had to be. I can choose the easy way! The life I grew up with was hard and beyond my control, but as an adult, I can choose for life to be easier than it was growing up.

It took courage to make the choice for an easier life. Courage to recognize that patterns developed in hardship and struggle no longer fit my life. Courage to believe I deserve an easy life and then to make the choices to support it. Courage to be selfish and demanding and confident in my pursuit of an easy life.

So, what if life is easy? Where can you find or create more ease in all you do? Instead of following your old habits, old beliefs, and old patterns, what if you challenged the idea that life is hard and, instead, chose to follow the ease?

Part 3:
Create

What do I want?

For years I struggled to get by and then to get to a sustainable level of happiness and success. In my thirties, for the first time in my life, I felt like I had "made it." I had secure employment and strong career prospects, was married to a genuinely good person, and my mental and emotional health were stable. For quite a few more years I was okay right where I was, solidly in the middle class.

The truth is, while I had a pretty good life, I was playing small. For years I didn't start the business I dreamed of having. I ignored the suggestion of a mentor and joined an open Toastmasters club instead of joining the advanced group I was invited to join. Frustrated with the lack of support from medical professionals, I accepted chronic physical pain and lived with chronic illnesses. Life was good—good enough.

What are you tolerating in your life? Is it something you want to continue to live with? Is your life "good enough?" You get to decide what kind of life you want to live—and whatever choice you make is okay—but this is the point when I challenge you to look inside and really ask yourself, "What do I want?" Are you living the life you want, or living for others? Are you following the path of least resistance, living the life you think you "should" want, or doing what other people have told you is right for you?

You can be happier and more fulfilled than you ever dreamed possible. You've come this far—look at all the amazing things you've done! Are you ready to see just how amazing your life can be?

The Shame of Need

My family wasn't always poor. We weren't wealthy, either, but for a few years of my life we lived somewhere between working class and middle class.

My mom was a single parent when she joined the Army, the quintessential *Private Benjamin* without the wealthy upbringing. I was six years old when my mom got her first duty assignment. My sister and I loaded all our Earthly possessions into my mom's wood-paneled station wagon and drove from Colorado to Alabama, singing along to a cassette tape of songs from our favorite Disney movies.

We didn't stay in Alabama long and moved next to Texas, where my mom fell in love and married her drill sergeant. My stepfather was the one transferred this time, and me, my sister, and pregnant mother followed him to Bramsche, Germany.

The three years we lived in Germany were some of the best and worst years of my life. I loved living in Germany, learning about the culture and going on adventures around the countryside. My mom stayed at home, cooking hearty meals, coming up with fun family craft projects, and sewing most of our clothes. We had a VCR and an Atari 2600, marking access to the resources money provides and some sense of security that got me through the times my life wasn't as safe or stable. During that same time, my alcoholic stepfather drank so much he regularly vomited blood, and his uneven temper could be terrifying. My night terrors started while we were in Germany, and I suffered the worst of all of my sexual abuse at the hands of a family friend and neighbor. Despite personal trauma, the benefits from the financial stability were obvious, especially after my stepfather retired from the Army and we moved back to Colorado.

My stepfather remained unemployed for years, struggling to find a job in the private sector while my mom supported the family working as a licensed practical nurse. At eleven years old I was too young to know the details of our financial situation, but what I do remember is we were poor. Poor enough to receive a donated turkey and basket of canned food for Thanksgiving. Poor enough that our names hung on the Giving Tree at the mall in hopes a charitable stranger would buy us the Christmas presents my parents couldn't afford.

The gift I received—She-Ra: Princess of Power and her winged unicorn Swift Wind—was very much wanted, but once I held

The Shame of Need

the plastic doll in my hands, it didn't feel as special as the handmade doll clothes from my mom. This gift from a stranger made me feel worthless. I felt judgement given with every bit of food and assistance we received: If my family wasn't poor, we wouldn't need help; if we just tried harder, we wouldn't be poor; if we were better people, we wouldn't be needy. The messages I learned at a young age were that being poor meant there was something wrong with us, and that receiving was shameful and weak.

I was a young girl when I resolved not to need anything from anyone. I would work hard for everything I had. I cut myself off from receiving help, gifts, money, favors, you name it. If I didn't earn it, I rejected it.

Sometimes I had no choice but to rely on others, and some of the time the charitable givers subtly, or not-so-subtly, condescended or shamed me for needing help. Each time I accepted help only if I had no other choice, and each time I renewed my commitment to being completely self-sufficient. Whenever possible, I found a way to pay back any gifts or favors in kind. I didn't want to need and I didn't want to receive.

I felt too much like being needy was a weakness, and too many times I heard people talk derisively about handouts and positively about the virtues of hard work, bootstrapping, and doing without. Maybe you heard these things too. Maybe you heard the message that it's wrong or bad to need. Maybe you were told it's better to earn what you have than to be given those things, or maybe you internalized the adage that it's better to give than to receive. As a woman, you probably learned it is shameful to receive—receiving is too close to needing and women who need too much are described as "clingy" and "insecure." So, you give and give and give some more. As a result of all this giving, you learned not to think too highly of yourself, to be humble, to be quiet, to be small. Other people shouldn't see whether or not you need anything. (You *don't* need anything, needing is bad, receiving is bad even though someone must be receiving everything you're giving.)

Could this be why you are uncomfortable receiving attention, compliments, or praise? Even basic acknowledgment can be hard to receive when you don't want anyone to think poorly of you. If your boss praises your efforts and you brush it off with a lackluster, "oh, it was nothing," then other people (including you) start to believe it really was nothing. When you respond to a compliment with a distracted "thank you," the compliment is forgotten as quickly as it came.

> **Here's the truth: As a human being, you need.**

The fear is that if you truly receive what is given to you, you might discover you're needy, prideful, or vain. Those are terrifying things to be when you've fought so hard to be none of those things! Here's the truth: As a human being, you need. You benefit from receiving. And the more you receive, the more you have to give. You've been carrying this shame around neediness with you for too long. Consider instead: what if receiving isn't shameful at all? What if receiving is essential to living your best life?

My Free Car

A few months after a friend moved to Colorado, her car broke down. Repairs would cost more than the car was worth and, with the recent moving expense, replacing her car wouldn't be possible either. For a few weeks she depended on rides from friends and coworkers. Relying on other people to get where you need to go is not a comfortable position to be in, but what else could she do?

As it turned out, one of her coworkers had an extra family car they didn't drive much and her coworker thought, why not give the car to someone who needed it? Because of their generosity, my friend paid $1 for a used Subaru Outback in good condition. She was basically given a free car!

I was relieved when my friend had a working car, as I'd been one of the people giving her rides, and as much as I  was happy to help my friend, I was glad to have one less person to consider in my daily routine. While I felt relieved, I also felt no small amount of angst over my friend's free car. I couldn't fathom the idea of being given a car, or of accepting a free car from a coworker. I struggled with it for weeks. I lay in bed at night, confounded, trying to put the thought out of my head. "How does someone give someone else a free car," I wondered. "How does someone receive a free car?" The thought made me uncomfortable, sitting in my stomach like a big rock, so I decided I needed to explore it further.

I worked on deepening my practice of receiving, playing with the idea of receiving and all that it entails. I pondered *receiving* a free car, still unable to feel comfortable being given such a big gift. One day during my daily meditation I imagined being open to receiving a free car. I visualized openly receiving a free car, gratefully accepting it into my life and my being.

"Okay, universe," I thought, determined, "I am open to receiving a car." I sat with that thought for a few minutes and nearly burst out laughing when I imagined Oprah standing in front of me in a gold-buttoned blazer, her head tilted back as she pointed at me, shouting, "You get a car!"

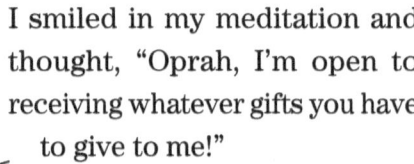

I smiled in my meditation and thought, "Oprah, I'm open to receiving whatever gifts you have to give to me!"

Wouldn't it be great if the next part of my story was telling you how I received a free car? That hasn't happened (yet), but after meditating and expanding my comfort with receiving, I am no longer kept up at night thinking about my friend's free car. If someone did give me a car, I just might be able to receive it with gratitude and grace. I won't feel guilty or undeserving. Wouldn't that be something?!

Learning to receive is not easy—especially for people who haven't enjoyed much privilege. If you haven't had a lot of experience in the area of receiving, you might, like me, bristle at the idea of getting something you haven't worked hard to earn. But to me it's not worth staying stuck, playing small, and struggling every day just to prove I've earned and continue to deserve my "hardship" badge. It's taken me a long time, but I've finally learned I don't need to work so hard for everything I receive. I don't need to prove myself. I don't need to earn everything. Can you be open to receiving whatever gifts come your way?

> But to me it's not worth staying stuck, playing small...

Receiving Is Better than Giving

All my life I have worked hard for everything I have. I am dedicated and motivated and I get shit done. My hard work and work ethic has lead to my success, no doubt. Yet I can look around at the world and see deserving people who don't get what they deserve and less-deserving people who have more than they need.

Throughout my career, I've seen the worst employees promoted and the best employees overlooked. Lazy and incompetent coworkers somehow managed to keep their jobs when better employees were fired. I've spent most of my life and my career proving myself to the world, so that when I have success, no one can say I didn't deserve it. But what if what I get is not directly related to how deserving I am? What if the difference between those with jobs and those let go has nothing to do with their work ethic? What if all I have to do is shift my mindset from proving myself to being open to receive? What if the real secret to getting more is *wanting* more?

With my old way of thinking I wasn't comfortable receiving unless I felt I deserved it. If someone tried to give me a free car, for example, I might reject it. Looking back on my life and career, I noticed there were times I was offered opportunities that I didn't accept because I believed I hadn't earned them.

This realization hit me when I listened to a friend and bodyworker talking about the small gifts and tokens of appreciation given to her by her clients. As I listened, I began to feel uncomfortable.

"My clients don't give me gifts," I thought as my discomfort grew. "Do her clients like her more than my clients like me? Am I not that good at what I do? Is that why my clients don't give me gifts?"

"Well, I guess it doesn't matter anyway," I thought, resolved. "I don't actually like it when people give me gifts."

BOOM.

I didn't want my clients to give me small gifts and tokens of appreciation because I didn't want gifts I hadn't earned or didn't deserve. Wasn't their payment appreciation enough? Oh, the horror, to think I might not just be needy, but that I might also be greedy.

Until that moment, I never realized exactly how uncomfortable I felt receiving. I saw the price tag attached to every exchange and I wondered if I'd given enough to deserve what I was receiving. But what might happen if I stopped trying so hard to prove myself and instead simply received more? What if I received *before* I gave? What if I filled myself up, up, up with all the best things in life and then used that abundance to give back to the world (instead of the other way around)? What if I'm already deserving and there's nothing more I have to do?

> What if I'm already deserving and there's nothing more I have to do?

Processing those questions has lead me to my most challenging lesson this past year—and the one that has contributed the most to my business success—learning it is better to RECEIVE than to GIVE.

I was raised to believe the opposite is true—that it is better to give than to receive. It was a belief that became so ingrained I became the ultimate giver. I gave to everyone and everything. I gave and gave and gave. I was so busy giving, I never really learned to receive. In fact, I sucked at receiving. I felt uncomfortable when I was given gifts, sometimes so much so that I gave the gift away to someone else so I didn't have to receive it. If a friend offered to pay for lunch, I argued, and then insisted on paying next time. When a friend helped me move, I made gesture after gesture to repay their efforts, from buying food to being the first person to show up whenever they needed help in the future.

I'm still so bad at receiving that I even deflect compliments. On the rare occasion I accept a compliment, I immediately return the compliment with gratitude, so I don't really have to embrace the original compliment. If someone compliments my appearance, I turn it around, so it sounds something like this, "Oh, thank you. That color green really brings out your eyes—you look so lovely today." Maybe, sometimes, I'll accept appreciation if I know I really, really, really earned it.

I measure my worth by how much I give. I am willing to go above and beyond for you, but I don't need much help, thanks. Receiving is a practice I'm only comfortable with as part of an exchange, and you'll probably get more from me than you give. I only want what's fair, and maybe even then I'll still feel a little guilty for whatever I get.

You see what I mean? I suck at receiving. But why do I suck at it so much? Well, let's start by exploring what it means to receive.

As defined by Merriam-Webster's online dictionary, as a verb, *receive* has several meanings:

1: to come into possession of

2: to act as a receptacle or container for

3a: to permit to enter: admit

   b: welcome, greet

   c: to react to in a specified manner

4: to accept as authoritative, true, or accurate: believe

5a: to support the weight or pressure of : bear

   b: to take (a mark or impression) from the weight of something

By that definition, in order to receive I have to come into possession of your appreciation. Worse yet, I have to act as a receptacle or container for your admiration. I have to admit and welcome your praise. I have to believe your compliments and accept them as truth. I have to support the weight of your gratitude.

Honestly, that sounds like a lot of work.

So if receiving is so much work, why do you have to learn how to do it? Why is receiving such an important skill?

Because to be successful in life you have to receive. You need to be comfortable receiving appreciation from bosses, clients, and colleagues. You need to be comfortable receiving tips and bonuses for a job well done. You need to be comfortable receiving awards, accolades, and other recognition for doing the awesome work you do. You have to believe that appreciation and success is true. You have to allow other people's admiration to bolster you—to embolden you! You have to receive so you can move forward even when you're scared. So you feel encouraged to take the next big leap. So you can stretch the limits of your comfort zone and grow into your full potential.

▸ Receiving is the key to a better life.

Own Your Awesome

It's difficult for women to receive praise for a number of reasons. You might be used to being overlooked at work, taken for granted at home, or trained to be humble, be silent, and not be a bother. As a result, women have a bad habit of deflecting compliments.

This phenomenon of deflection works like a game of dodgeball—you see the compliment coming and at the last second you jump and contort your body to avoid being hit.

> **This phenomenon of deflection works like a game of dodgeball.**

Compliment dodgeball happens when you're praised at work and you downplay your contribution, aka the Thanks, but.

- Thanks, but I wasn't happy with the font I used.
- Thanks, but I barely finished on time.
- Thanks, but it was not my best work.
- Thanks, but it was a team effort.

Don't be a but-head. Here's how to respond instead:

- Thanks, I am proud of my contribution to this project.

- Thank you. Would you mind passing that feedback on to my boss?
- Thank you. (End stop.)

Another form of compliment dodgeball happens when you justify the compliment to prove you really deserve the credit, aka I'm Actually Really Qualified!

- Thank you! My masters degree finally paid off!
- Thank you! I worked all weekend to get it done!
- Thank you! Writing this book has been a long and difficult process!

Instead of justifying praise, try receiving it. Thank you is all you really need to say.

Yet another form of compliment dodgeball happens when you barely register praise before giving it right back, aka I'm Rubber and You're Glue.

- Oh, thank you! And you did such a great job leading that meeting last week.
- Thank you! And thank you for the yummy cookies you brought in yesterday.
- Thanks! And you're such a great person. You have great hair.

Sure, it's nice and polite to return a compliment with a compliment, but it's also a great way to avoid letting the original compliment sink in.

Own Your Awesome

If you want to develop advanced receiving skills with accepting compliments, try this: Find a friend, or a group of friends, and practice receiving compliments. Make an agreement that whenever you are complimented by your friend, you reply, "Thank you, I know."

Saying "I know" in response to a compliment will be difficult. It feels like the opposite of humility because it not only receives the praise, it reinforces it as something you admit about yourself. You may have been told that knowing you're good at something is actually bad—it's arrogant, it's vain, it's conceited. But here's the thing—it's not bad to know what you're good at. It's actually *good* to know how you shine. Knowing where you excel, and actually receiving positive feedback, contributes to being chosen for amazing opportunities, getting paid on par with your male counterpart, and building trust and credibility. And it's how you bolster confidence and believe in yourself!

If "thank you, I know" is too difficult as a starting point, try saying "thank you, I believe you" in response to compliments and praise. Get comfortable with "thank you, I believe you," and then move on to practicing "thank you, I know." Stop minimizing, justifying, and deflecting compliments and praise. Receive praise instead and own your awesome!

Living with Intention

Growing up in my home there wasn't a lot of stability. Every evening I had to wonder, would my alcoholic stepfather lash out in a drunken rage, or would we have a fun night playing family board games? When I got home from school, which of my mom's multiple personalities would I face? Had my mom been admitted to the psych ward, or would we snuggle up on the couch and watch *Star Trek: The Next Generation*? Would the phone get shut off? Would we get evicted? I lived so much of my life in survival mode, on alert for the next crisis, that I never felt safe.

Regardless of your circumstances, maybe you can relate to never feeling quite secure, to not knowing what will go wrong next, or to waiting for the other shoe to drop. Expecting and then reacting to the latest disaster may sound like a regular part of your life. Never feeling rested or being able to let your guard down may be your status quo. Living like this, constantly reacting, adjusting, or recovering from what happens around you is living in survival mode. Survival mode can be triggered by any kind of significant life stress—from the day-to-day stress of poverty to the emotional trauma of job loss, divorce, or death. Living in survival mode

> Expecting and then reacting to the latest disaster may sound like a regular part of your life.

for an extended period of time can turn those survival instincts into habit, making you tense, anxious, and reactive, even when things are okay. Those habits of reacting to life—especially when you've experienced trauma or have been limited by socioeconomic factors—can continue and negatively affect you when you're trying to create something bigger and better for yourself.

Learning to live, not just survive, takes time and, likely, more than a little therapy. I was in and out of therapy for many years learning healthy behaviors and coping skills, some of which are featured in this book. As I learned new skills, I had more options for dealing with stress. These new skills allowed me to create more happiness and security in my life. In my early-to-mid thirties I began responding to my life differently. I practiced living intentionally instead of moving through life reacting to what was happening around me.

Living intentionally requires you to make choices rather than react. Here's an example: One morning I woke tired and groggy and had trouble getting going. It was snowing, too, which meant I had to change the outfit I'd laid out the night before. A blanket of fresh snow slowed traffic considerably and, with all the delays, I was getting later and later by the second.

When I arrived at work late, I might have called it a bad day and held on to a bad mood and negative mindset, but I didn't. I wasn't about to have a bad day on account of a few small setbacks. Later that day, I arrived home to a burst pipe and a flooded family room. Okay, *now* I was having a bad day—but I wasn't, really. We were

Living With Intention

fortunate the flooding happened during a remodel and our furniture and valuables were out of the room. The sopping wet carpet was the old carpet we intended to replace anyway. I admit I felt a little bit of stress over dealing with the cleanup, but the damage was minimal. This was a situation I could handle.

By putting my situation in perspective, I was able to deal with all the inconveniences and still have an okay day. Perspective is everything! I could have easily gotten caught up in the day's challenges instead of deciding what kind of day I wanted to have and using healthy tools to shape my experience.

Living with intention is when you have a purpose and a plan, and you actively make choices that support you. You choose to respond instead of react. You become empowered and begin to make choices that consider your life as a whole instead of reacting to what is happening in the moment. Living intentionally means you are purposeful in word and action. It means you live a life that is meaningful and fulfilling to you. It means you make thoughtful choices that support your happiness and well-being. It doesn't mean you never react—even after years of therapy, growth, and personal development, it sometimes still takes a bit of practice to quiet that survival instinct and live with intention. But it does mean you have the tools to take a beat, realign your perspective, and make a more intentional choice.

> **Make choices that consider your life as a whole instead of reacting to what is happening in the moment.**

Living with intention asks you to:

Respond instead of react.

Love instead of fear.

Embrace instead of expect.

Accept instead of resist.

Be intentional because you want to do more than just get by. Be intentional because you dream. Because you aspire. Because you care. Because you live.

Sure, it's easy to do what others do. For example, it's easy to complain about Mondays because that's what other people do. What if, instead, you actively, intentionally chose to wake up excited about the day? How does that change your outlook? How does that affect your day at work? Your interactions? Your mood? That's the power of living with intention.

Here are a few ways to live with intention:

Choose

Remind yourself you have choices—lots of choices—more choices than you can think of when you're reactive. Make a list of all the possible choices you could make. Avoid acting out of habit, and instead make a choice you've never tried before. Ask yourself, "What do I choose?"

Desire

Desire motivates and inspires the best in you. Desire can inform actionable steps to create a better life. Every day, every activity, everything you do, ask yourself, "What do I want to get out of this? What experience do I want to have? What outcome do I desire?"

Wonder

Be actively curious how situations might work out. Stop assuming you know the outcome. Ask yourself, "What am I assuming?" Then ask, "What don't I know?" Curiosity allows situations to work out for the best. Be present in the wonder of the moment.

Agree or Disagree with Integrity

Say yes or say no with integrity. Only say yes if it's the right thing to do, when saying yes honors you. Say no when you can't or don't want to fulfill the request. Say no when the only reason to say yes is feeling like you "should." Go back and reread Chapter 15: How to Say No if needed.

Be Present

Stop living in the past, revisiting past pain. Avoid living in the future, worrying over situations that haven't happened yet. Be present, here and now. Right now you're safe and everything is okay. Taking three deep breaths is a simple, easy way to ground yourself in the present.

> **Right now you're safe and everything is okay.**

> Give living intentionally a try, and remember it's a practice, a way of life. When the shit hits the fan, you might still react. You have to choose, day after day, to live with intention. If you get off track, you can always come back to intention. Keep practicing, keep living the life you want to live.

Stand Up, Speak Up

Once I had created a better life for myself, I languished there. Life was better, sometimes good, occasionally great. I had so much more than I grew up with and this new level of privilege stretched ingrained ideas about what I deserved and what I could achieve. But I listened to the inner voice of self-doubt, fear, and shame from my past and didn't live up to my full potential. I challenged myself to only meet the greatness of my average peers. Until one day, I didn't.

> I challenged myself to only meet the greatness of my average peers. Until one day, I didn't.

That day happened on a clear January morning. I sat in a hotel meeting room on the last day of speaker training—one of the in-person events for the business coaching program I enrolled in when I started my business. That morning we were given the opportunity to get on stage one last time. There wasn't enough time for everyone to speak, so we would only be hearing from volunteers. When they announced the final "get up," I longed to participate, but before I stood up, I heard the nagging voice of self-doubt.

"Who do you think you are? You don't want anyone here to think you're full of yourself. You're no better than anyone else here," the voice insisted. "Give someone else a chance. Stay in your seat."

In the moment I hesitated, others lined up for their last chance to speak.

"Okay, that's all we'll have time for," the trainer announced. "We'll finish up with the people who are already in line."

As I watched each speaker on stage, I beat myself up a little more. "This is crazy," I thought. "I paid a lot of money to be here. I paid for a hotel. I took time off work. Why wouldn't I get up on stage one more time? Why shouldn't I?"

But it was too late. I became more frustrated with myself, watching from my chair at the end of the front row, right near the steps leading to the stage.

The second-to-last speaker was a tall, beautiful woman named Sarah. She walked toward the platform steps and hesitated. She suddenly changed direction and approached me.

Her warm brown eyes looked into mine. "I want you to take my place," she whispered.

I met her gaze, bewildered.

"I want to hear from you again, and I think you have something important to say," she continued.

I hesitated briefly, then stood up from my seat and resolutely walked up the steps and onto the stage. I stood on the stage, voice trembling as I told this story. I spoke of my desire to stand up and speak, of my self-doubt and missing my chance, and of Sarah's incredible offer to give up her spot.

"The last thing I expected was for Sarah to give up her spot for me," I said, "and I will not stay seated. I'm done playing small. I'm done keeping quiet. I will speak my truth and I will not let another opportunity pass me by."

I looked out and noticed I wasn't the only one with tears in my eyes. About half of the audience was crying. They were completely silent and all eyes were fixed on me.

That moment changed the course of my business and life. I wasn't going to stay seated anymore. I wasn't going to regret not getting up.

Life is rarely fair. Most of us won't have opportunities handed to us. We won't have a Sarah who sees our potential and gives up her spot for us. We have to find opportunities, create opportunities, and we have to fucking stand up and take opportunities when they are offered to us.

After that lesson at speaker training, I started to challenge myself to go big and bigger. I challenged my discomfort with just how much better life could be. Could it better than this? Can I allow myself to have even more? I started taking bigger risks and being bolder in my business. I'll be honest, I was—and am—scared shitless most of the time. And I'm not going to let that stop me. I have something important to say, and the world wants to hear more from me.

I want you to start standing up and speaking up. What's stopping you? Where in your life are you playing small? I want you to start showing up for your life in bigger ways. You have something important to say, and there is someone out there who wants to hear from you. The world needs what you have to offer. The world needs your contribution, your voice, especially because you have faced great challenges. The world needs to be inspired and your story is inspiring. It's your turn to stand up and speak.

> **It's your turn to stand up and speak.**

Desires on Fire

I first noticed my disconnection from desire in my early twenties while participating in a sexual assault survivors group for women. Our meetings started with a check-in question, "How are you feeling?" Even with the list of emotions at the back of our group book, I struggled to define any emotion beyond happy, sad, or depressed. Week after week I carefully read through the list, reading each emotion and asking myself, "Is this what I feel?" Sometimes reading the word was enough for me to recognize it as what I was feeling. Other weeks I read through the list of emotions several times before choosing one that might be what I was feeling.

Being a survivor of sexual assault contributed to my disconnection with myself, and so did living in poverty for so many years. Surviving meant all my focus had to be on the next crisis, on being hypervigilant to what might break or go wrong. That didn't leave space for me to consider what I wanted beyond praying for something to *not* be in crisis. When we were poor, there wasn't enough money to extend beyond the most essential items. At some point, with all this focus on just getting by, I stopped considering what I wanted because I probably

> **Beyond the basics for survival, I didn't know what I wanted...**

wasn't going to get it anyway. For most of my life, up through young adulthood, I was disconnected from desire. Beyond the basics for survival, I didn't know what I wanted, particularly when what I wanted affected another person.

A fairly common question when making dinner plans is "Where do you want to go for dinner?" Most people might have a ready response, but my default reply was "Oh, anything is fine with me. I'm flexible." I kept putting the decision back on the other person, not only because I didn't know what I wanted, but because I didn't want to be in conflict with what they wanted.

Living in Colorado, I've often been asked if I enjoy hiking, and this simple question often vexed me. I didn't know how to respond. The truth is I don't actually like hiking. It feels like something I *should* enjoy, but I don't. Even so, I've been more likely to respond, "You know, I haven't been hiking in a while but I'm adventurous and up for anything." I don't want to *offend* the person asking. Hiking is a perfectly fine activity, but my response undermines my ability to clearly identify and speak to my own interests. It suppresses my desire. (Before you ask, I don't like camping either.)

I can relate my disconnection from emotions, including desire, to my history. But I know other women, with different histories from complex and varied backgrounds, who also struggle to suggest a restaurant to meet a friend for dinner or who suppress their desires in favor of someone else's. I know more women than men who are challenged to express their opinions and preferences. In my experience, it's less common to find a man who stumbles answering a simple question like, "where do you want to eat," or "what movie do you want to see," and even less common for a man to keep his opinion to himself in a business meeting or other professional context. Women specifically seem unused to knowing, let alone expressing, their own desires. Women aren't encouraged to want or to desire.

Many of the women I coach experience this lack of desire. While they can safely feel and express socially acceptable desires, to have a good marriage or to be financially secure, they struggle to know what's next for them in their business or career. They have spent their life and career following a traditional path, only to find themselves overworked, unfulfilled, and underpaid.

As I work with these women, I often find they have a hidden desire, some big dream they haven't given themselves permission to believe in. Perhaps they believed it when someone told them their dream was impossible. Or maybe because they don't know how to pursue their dream, they convinced themselves they can't have it. Impostor syndrome may tell them they don't know enough or haven't earned the chance to go after what they really want. Or, some of these women may be like me, feeling like they don't deserve more. When a dream is dampened, any and all of these reasons can lead to a shutdown of desire.

What do you want? It is such a short, simple question and yet it can be so hard to answer. Do you know what you want? Are you comfortable expressing your desire? How is a lack of desire impacting your life? Maybe your biggest and boldest dreams have been squashed by what the world expects from you. Maybe they've been squashed to the point you have forgotten how to dream. Have you, too, been conditioned to accommodate, to consider everyone else's interests before your own, to believe that anyone and everyone else knows better than you do—even when it relates to your own interests?

Maybe, like me, you began to explore what you want, beyond those wants that are expected and commercially approved, and it's still difficult to ask for what you want. Like my relationship with the business consultant I fired, you may not realize your needs aren't being met until it's too late. Perhaps you attempt to set boundaries only after your boundary has already been crossed.

> Light your desire on fire so that what you want burns inside of you and lights your way.

The key to changing this dynamic in yourself, and in society, is to become familiar with your desire. Know what you truly want so you can begin to ask for it and even demand it. Light your desire on fire so that what you want burns inside of you and lights your way. Your desire is powerful. Let it motivate you. Let it fuel you.

A good place to start building your desire is by asking yourself, "What do I want?" Ask this question, and then listen to the answer. Notice what you feel in your body as you ask what you want. Does some part of your body feel tight, constricted, or stuck? Do you feel it in your jaw, neck, throat, stomach, or some other part? Does your body feel relaxed, strong, open, or excited? Do you resist the question? Is there a part of you longing to shout an answer? This exercise may be challenging at first. You may not know what you want. But keep asking yourself the question to illuminate what you want and to practice thinking about what you want.

Ask yourself what you want in social settings, too. When you're deciding where to meet a group of friends for dinner or what movie to see, ask yourself what you want to do. Ask what you want when the hostess at a restaurant inquires, "Is this table okay?" Well, is it? Expressing your desire starts with recognizing your desire, even if you choose to go along with whatever the group decides.

Always ask yourself what you want at work or when you're offered a job. "What do I want? Do I want this responsibility? Do I want this salary?" Pro tip: you don't have to agree to whatever is being offered to you.

> **Pro tip: you don't have to agree to whatever is being offered to you.**

Asking for what you want, as scary as it is, is often effective. Also, asking for what you want at work rarely sounds as selfish, arrogant, greedy, needy, or rude as you might think it does.

Ask yourself what you want when you're surrounded by family. Ask yourself even when the question hasn't been asked to you and it's assumed you'll go along with whatever someone else wants. Keep the question in mind during every decision so you are always in connection with your desire. Whether or not you decide to act on your desire, please, at least know what you desire in any and every situation!

Give yourself permission to desire more. Hold the charge of your desire. Connect your feelings to your desire. How does happiness, heartbreak, anger, or loneliness affect what you want? Emotions are powerful influencers. Ask yourself, "Given how I'm feeling, what is it that I want?"

Keep asking. Keep listening. As you find it easier to connect to your desire, be bold enough to ask for what you want. If you need a refresher on asking for what you want, refer back to Chapter 17: Be Awesomely Selfish and Chapter 18: Be Demanding.

Know what you want. Ask for what you want. Get what you want, at least a little more often. Light your desire on fire and let your desire guide you.

Self-Trust and Building Intuition

All people are intuitive beings. You are intuitive. I am intuitive. Even when my intuition was warped by my circumstances, and I didn't recognize my intuition for what it is, I was still intuitive.

I identify as highly sensitive—a quality I believe comes from having a high level of intuition.

> You are intuitive.

When I walk into a store, I notice every detail—the colors, the lights, the textures, the sounds. I notice details other people don't. I can tell people's moods by looking at them. I notice their joys and frustrations. I'm so good at reading people I've been playfully accused of reading minds. I often instantly like or dislike certain people (a gut feeling). I can get easily overwhelmed by too much sensory input, and I dislike shopping at stores that aren't visually well-organized.

I can't say how much of this sensitivity comes naturally and how much of my intuition was honed as a survival instinct from constantly feeling unsafe in childhood. This high level of insight created anxiety and sometimes allowed me to avoid or defuse volatile situations in my childhood home. Even though I could use my intuition to positively affect my environment, my perceptions were consistently undermined. Many of the adults around me told me what I saw, felt, heard, and believed was wrong.

••

> "Shhh…don't cry." (Your feelings are inappropriate.)
>
> "I'll give you something to cry about." (Your feelings are invalid.)
>
> "It's okay, you can trust me." (Trust what you're told, not what you feel.)
>
> "Go on, give your uncle a hug." (What other people want is more important than your discomfort.)
>
> "Children are to be seen and not heard." (Your thoughts and feelings don't matter.)

••

I learned not to put much stock in my own thoughts, feelings, or intuition. This lead to severe confusion and mistrust of myself when it was actually other people who were not to be trusted. This conditioning carried into adulthood, where the pattern continued at my first job.

My first job out of high school, as a retail clerk at one of the top ten largest department stores, seemed like a cool job—at least it was better than working fast food. I had some great coworkers, made some friends, and got a decent store discount. But despite what I thought was an impeccable work ethic, I consistently butted heads with upper management. On one such day, an

Self-Trust and Building Intuition

older female executive manager spotted me standing in a furniture aisle.

"What are you doing?" she asked.

"I'm waiting for Mark to come help me lift these boxes." I pointed to a stack of unassembled furniture boxes with bright red stickers that read "TEAM LIFT," a safety sticker reminding employees that two team members were required to meet safety code.

She rolled her eyes and sneered, "Stop standing around and move it yourself."

In this top-down culture, I, as the subordinate employee, was subservient to her, the boss, and my safety needs were not important. Despite knowing better, that manager belittled and demeaned me for following the safety policy. This same executive manager later interfered when I applied for a team lead position, suggesting I was a troublemaker and was "not a team player." I started to wonder if being a good employee would require me to do what I was told, not what I knew was right.

Ah, I remembered this lesson from childhood. With so many people in positions of trust and authority telling me I was wrong so much of the time, it was no wonder I found it difficult to trust myself!

As I got older, I stopped putting so much importance on what other people told me

WHO DO YOU TRUST?

and started to increase my trust in my experience and intuition. I acted on my intuition more and more, but I still looked for outward verification that I was right. After years of not trusting myself, I wanted someone to agree with or approve of my intuition. I sought validation, talking about my decisions with friends and coworkers. If I couldn't get verbal validation, I checked the results of the decision. I viewed success as proof that my intuition was trustworthy, and saw failure as proof that I was wrong all along.

The truth—my truth—is that any action comes with both positive and negative consequences. While sometimes those consequences are more extreme than others, what I experience is largely dependent on my perspective. I can choose to focus on the positives, and take that positive outlook as proof that I did the right thing in trusting myself, or I can choose to focus on the negatives, and take that negative outlook as proof that I am inherently untrustworthy, just like all those people have been telling me for years.

It took me a while to understand how my outlook factors into my evaluations, but now that I understand it, I can say with certainty that my truth also tells me my intuition is trustworthy. I have far more to gain and far more to offer this world by trusting myself and my intuition than I do by believing people who are unhappy, irritable, or have their own best interests at heart. I have far more to gain and far

> I have far more to gain and far more to offer this world by trusting myself and my intuition...

more to offer this world by trusting myself and my intuition than I do by believing others who haven't lived my experience, who don't know me, and who may not have my best interests at heart. I have my best interests at heart, not at the expense of others, but in support of myself and my own well-being.

Rise To The Challenge

On a sunny Colorado afternoon in February, I attended an educational session at Startup Week, a week-long community event for business owners and entrepreneurs. The presenter was a congenial white man with a blonde beard and deep voice, wearing a buttoned cardigan sweater over his dress shirt. He spoke with the smooth cadence of an old-time radio narrator.

The session was interactive and informative, and as I engaged with the presenter and other audience members, I became intrigued and wanted to know more about the services his company provided. When he finished his presentation, he opened the floor for questions.

I had lots of questions! Some clients had asked me for recommendations that aligned with the services he provided, so I wanted to know more specifics about his clientele and about his programs supporting local business owners and business leaders. Specifically I asked how many of his members were women business owners and how many advisors in his programs were female.

My questions hit a nerve.

He stammered his responses, explaining that the numbers weren't as good as they'd like. He guessed 25–30% of their members were female and defended those numbers saying, "But it doesn't have much of an impact because the issues faced by women and men in these businesses are similar—they face similar challenges. Actually, I consider myself gender agnostic."

Feelings of frustration and anger bubbled to the surface at the blatant mansplaining.

"That has not been my experience," I countered. "May I challenge you on this?"

He nodded.

"In my experience as a woman, as a career coach, and as the founder of a women's organization, I have found that there are nuances and biases in business that affect women differently than men. For example, did you know that less than 3% of investor funding is granted to women-owned businesses? It's much harder for women business owners to get funded."

"Well, that doesn't really apply here," he said with authority. "None of the members in my programs are in the startup phase. The issues my members face are the same, regardless of gender."

He continued, completely dismissing my comments

and concerns by saying, "Actually, I don't believe in women-only organizations. Women need the perspective of men to be successful in business. We need each other's perspectives."

After contradicting his stance of being "gender agnostic," he quickly ended the session fifteen minutes early.

I walked out of the session frustrated and uninspired. What had started as an interesting educational event had devolved into yet another example of a privileged individual disregarding and minimizing the challenges of a less-privileged group.

I could have held on to those negative feelings and let my disappointment eat at me, but, nervous and outraged, I posted about my experience publicly on my Facebook page. My heartfelt and passionate post gained the attention of community members and the organizers of Startup Week, with more than sixty comments within twenty-four hours. Because I had the courage to speak up, I started a conversation in my local business community about the specific challenges women face, and how events like Startup Week can be more inclusive and supportive to women.

Just a year before, I don't think I would have challenged the presenter the way I did, and I certainly would not have posted about it publicly. Speaking up at this event was scary for me, and posting my experience publicly was

> It's time to find my voice. It's time to speak my truth.

terrifying. It would have been easy to just vent to a few close friends, but speaking up started a conversation that will lead to more awareness and inclusion. I was, and am, extremely nervous about speaking up. But I know it's time. It's time to find my voice. It's time to speak my truth.

Every time I speak up, I am empowered and encouraged. I feel my courage, my confidence, and my authority. Every time I speak up, it's easier to speak up the next time, and the next. It's time to challenge the status quo.

Another amazing thing happens when I speak up: I empower and encourage the people around me. I inspire others to speak up for themselves. I motivate them to speak up for people other than themselves, too. We need to speak for ourselves and for others. It's your time. Find your voice. Claim your power. Speak your truth. Speak up. The world is listening. What do you have to say?

Progress Is the New Perfect

Throughout my life, as I worked to improve myself and my situation, I was nagged by the feeling that I wasn't good enough. Because I hadn't achieved my goals, hadn't become "good enough," I couldn't stop to relax or allow myself to be happy or enjoy life in the moment. Just like when I threw my paper in the garbage for getting a B, for much of my life I fcused on getting things "right." Progress didn't inform my worth because it wasn't complete, and therefore what I was working toward wasn't "right" yet.

A few months ago a coaching client sat in my office, fidgeting in the chair across from me. "I keep thinking I'll finally be okay when I reach the next goal, but I keep moving the line. I get close to one goal, and then I find a new goal, pushing the mark farther and farther away. It's never enough. I'm never enough."

I knew this feeling well. I never felt I was good enough, and whenever I got close to my initial goal, to the thing I thought would finally make me feel good enough, I too pushed the goal line. There was always more work to do. Everything I did right was plagued by the things I did

> **You are enough.**

wrong. The feeling of not being enough pervaded my every action, just as it did so for my client. But that's bullshit—we are enough, and you are enough, too.

When you've lived with so much hardship, your viewpoint might be skewed toward the negative. It's that survival instinct I've talked about before. You become so attuned to the next crisis—watching, waiting, planning for things to go wrong—that you ignore or minimize things that are going right. The survival instinct tells you to be alert to danger. Being alert to anything else, even positive feelings, is contrary to that survival instinct.

But once the trauma is past, once you've begun the healing journey, this survival instinct harms more than it helps. It can make taking time out to celebrate and enjoy life feel foreign. Without the ability to recognize and celebrate progress—not just the big wins but the small ones, too—you may stay trapped in the cycle of struggle, discomfort, and pain. But when you can learn to see and enjoy the good stuff in life, it gives you the motivation and inspiration to level up in big ways.

When you're safe, when your life is stable, when things are generally going well, what you need most is to become attuned to success and to strengthen your ability to celebrate it. Like building your ability to be grateful, learning to acknowledge and enjoy your progress is a relatively simple skill that has significant advantages.

So, what does it look like to celebrate your progress? It starts with recognizing that you're making progress. It's easy to acknowledge an obvious benchmark for success, such as earning an MBA, hitting a certain salary, or taking your dream vacation. It's harder to acknowledge the progress you make toward those goals before you achieve the goal—but that is exactly what you should celebrate. Spend less time, energy, and attention focused on the outcome, and instead focus on the progress.

> Progress is the new perfect.

Some signs of progress might be completing a course requirement, setting a boundary at work, or even spending thirty minutes a day working on your goal. It's important to intentionally acknowledge this progress and build your ability to celebrate your progress. You can practice enjoying your progress in a variety of ways.

Report Your Weekly Wins

Report your big and small wins weekly in a journal. Or, better yet, share your weekly wins with a coach or accountability partner. When you're challenged to write down two or three wins each week, you start to notice both big and small signs of your progress.

Write it Down and Watch it Grow

Get a clear or translucent jar or container. Write down each accomplishment, each finished step, on a slip of paper and fill the jar with these signs of your progress. Because the container is see-through, at a glance you can see how much you've accomplished.

Celebrate Your Progress

Come up with a list of small rewards to celebrate each time you make progress or hit a new benchmark on a bigger goal. Your rewards list might include treating yourself to a meal at your favorite restaurant, buying a new pair of shoes, or putting twenty dollars in your dream vacation fund. Pick a reward from your list and reward yourself—actually reward yourself—every time you earn a reward. No, really, reward yourself for your hard work, you need to celebrate it!

Each of these practices can help you create a habit of attuning yourself to the good and recognizing when you make progress, especially when you haven't hit the big goals yet. This helps to keep your mindset positive and serves as a reminder that even if you haven't hit the goal, you're on the path. Progress is the new perfect.

I Ain't Got No Body

Of all the personal and professional development I've done, for years there was one big piece missing. That piece was my physical body. Most of the work I had done before my forties focused on healing my mental, emotional, and spiritual self. I spent years of my life in my head, disconnected from my body and disconnected from myself. Much of my life felt like an out-of-body experience. For years I struggled with chronic illness manifesting as inflammation, irritation, and pain throughout my body. Addressing my mental, emotional, and spiritual health slightly improved my physical health, but I still felt physically ill more days than not. I had a hate-hate relationship with my body. I felt at war with my body. I didn't trust my body. I didn't want to be in my body.

Time and again I tried to "figure it out." I saw doctor after doctor. I got blood tests, CT scans, and more tests. When my worry, anxiety, frustration, and stress took over my mind, I wasn't aware of my body, and the few times I was, I was usually only aware of it in the form of complaints. My neck hurt from the pain radiating from my clenched jaw. My shoulders seized from being habitually rounded in quiet shame. Emotion welled up and tightened my throat as I choked on my words. My stomach wrenched with anxiety.

I grew accustomed to those daily aches and pains caused by my mental state, but I was also frequently sick, adding to my disconnection with my physical self. Bronchitis, infections, vocal cord dysfunction, adult-onset asthma, chronic sinusitis, and acid reflux all chased me into my adulthood, furthering my distrust and dislike of my physical self. My body and I did not get along.

My physical self wasn't entirely neglected or hated. In high school I discovered one place where I could

let go of my stress and anxiety and inhabit my body: the dance studio. Before getting involved with dance, I always believed I was uncoordinated and unathletic. My body didn't seem to do things other people's bodies could do. Dance changed that for me. I studied tap and jazz through high school and into my early twenties. I felt alive in my body when I danced. For at least an hour a week, I could feel my body.

I had a similar experience when I started practicing yoga in my late twenties. Yoga allowed me to inhabit and engage my body, feeling muscles throughout my body from head to toe. It helped improve my mental, physical, emotional, and spiritual health. But then, after a series of health issues and seven major and minor surgeries, my ability to continue my yoga practice was greatly limited. I fell into old habits and avoided feeling my body.

During that time, I found I could connect to my body in limited and brief moments. Sometimes I would go for a walk and with each step I would notice the ground beneath my feet. I felt the way my feet connected to the earth and supported my body. From that attention, my creativity increased and stress decreased. Those walks allowed me to feel my body for a few minutes at a time, but maintaining this connection to my physical self quickly dissipated when I stopped moving and my energy and focus returned to my headspace.

I continued into my late thirties still somewhat disconnected from my physical body until I found the Art of Feminine Presence, a body of work focusing on being physically and energetically present in the body. (Spoilers: this practice was so helpful I am now a licensed teacher of the Art of Feminine Presence.)

Through these series of practices, I learned to be present in my body all of the time. I discovered new ways to engage in my physical body, to be present in and through myself. I learned to take up my space in the world—to know and feel the space that is mine. To my surprise, as I became more and more present in my body, my minor aches and pains lessened. When I was present and embodied in my entire physical body, I

> I learned to take up my space in the world—to know and feel the space that is mine.

realized those minor complaints were a small part of the whole me.

Through the Art of Feminine Presence I increased my awareness of my energetic body, discovering the electrical impulses flowing through me. I was illuminated like a light bulb. I allowed myself to shine brightly in the world. I became me—fully and completely me.

With this new ability to be physically and energetically present, I no longer walked into a room of strangers and wanted to be invisible. I became visible and, instead of feeling scary as I expected it would, being visible felt wonderful.

A few months after taking Art of Feminine Presence classes and practicing being present, I began to notice a difference, not only in how I felt, but also in how other people responded to me. When I stopped shrinking and hiding, I connected with people more easily. The change was undeniable during a quarterly business training. Other participants who had met me before were suddenly very interested in what I was doing in my business. I received invitations to lunches and dinners. Colleagues asked for my advice. I was confused and curious about this new attention. What changed, I wondered. That's when I realized what was different—me. I had been studying and practicing presence for several months and people were taking notice!

I noticed a change in how people responded to me every day, too. When I walked down the street, I no longer stepped off the sidewalk into gutters or rocky landscaping to avoid other people running into me. I took up my space, present in my body, and more often than not other people, particularly men, stepped to the side to accommodate me. In the beginning, the feeling of being present in my body felt unfamiliar. As I continued to practice this work, it began to feel natural and very enjoyable. I practiced weekly at first, then daily. Now any time I walk down the street I play with one of these practices, having fun increasing my presence and enjoying it more and more.

Want to try it for yourself? Here are some simple, easy exercises to increase your physical and energetic presence:

Wiggle Your Toes

You can't do it without thinking about your toes, can you? Wiggling your toes increases your awareness of your legs, feet, and toes. Many women energetically disconnect at the neck or waist. Feeling your toes brings your energy down through your body, and helps you feel more grounded. I tell my coaching clients to wiggle their toes during job interviews as it causes us to slow down and be present.

Practice Downward-Facing Dog

If you're physically able and have received previous professional instruction, practice the widely-recognized yoga pose downward-facing dog. Downward-facing dog is a standing forward bend, engaging muscles throughout your body. Feeling and stretching muscles in your hands, arms, back, legs, and feet brings attention, and you, into your physical body. (Please consult a medical professional before trying any exercise routine, and consult a yoga teacher for the best instruction on this pose.)

Breathe into Your Belly

Start this exercise by taking three deep breaths, allowing the first breath to fill your lungs, then drawing breath down into your torso, and then taking a third breath into your belly. As you inhale, allow your belly to be pushed outward like a pregnant belly. Keep breathing into your belly for two to three more minutes.

Engage Your Sacral Chakra

Close your eyes and take a few deep belly breaths. Focus your attention on the center of your pelvic bowl—for women this spot is about two to three inches below your belly button and two inches back toward your spine—this is your sacral chakra, the energetic point of your core associated with passion, creativity, and emotion. Imagine a point of light at your sacral chakra. Continue to focus on this light and notice how the light breathes with you. As you breathe in, the light expands. As you breathe out, the light contracts. Keep focusing your attention on this point of light for two to three minutes, feeling more and more present in your sacral chakra.

The energy anchoring in your body can be felt by others. When my energetic dog, a 65-pound Lab-Pitty-Dane mix, pulls on the leash during a walk, I engage my sacral chakra and the tension on the leash decreases as he responds to my anchoring energy.

Stir Up the Energy

Rub your hands together for thirty seconds, then hold your hands slightly apart. Notice the energy in, around, and through your hands. Imagine that energy flowing through your wrists, up your arms, into your shoulders, down into your chest, torso, and into your belly. See how long you can hold the charge of that energy in and through your body. Scan your body and if you notice any part is disconnected, gently rub that part of your body to stir up the energy.

Engage Your Senses

Engage all five senses in an everyday activity, such as washing the dishes. Notice the warmth as you plunge your hands into the soapy, hot water. Do you smell lemon in the dish soap? Can you imagine the flavor of the meal you last ate from the plate in your hand? Look at the small rainbows sitting on the edge of the soap bubbles. Listen to the clinking of the dishes as they scrape and collide in the sink. Notice your shoulders, your back, your legs, and your feet as you stand at the sink. What do you notice in your body as you work? Engaging your five senses is a simple, easy way to be more present to your body, in your body.

> **Engaging your five senses is a simple, easy way to be more present to your body, in your body.**

Being present can become so natural that you don't have to think about it—and that is quite the accomplishment for someone who has overcome great personal and social challenges. Too often we're far more aware of others than we are of ourselves. Like most of the wisdom shared in this book, being present in your body is a practice, and with regular practice it takes less conscious thought and effort. Practice makes progress!

Find Your Community

When I was a little girl, I made an important choice to create a better life for myself. I attribute my success in achieving this goal to my own hard work and self motivation. The main difference between me and other members of my family raised in similar circumstances is not talent or skill, it's sheer determination. I was determined to succeed, and so I did. That tenacity, that drive, it came from within.

And yet, I didn't succeed alone. I succeeded with the help of others. Community is essential, and with the support of the right people, I can accomplish far more than I ever could have alone. Throughout my adult life I have found communities of people, and within those communities I gained the courage, love, and acceptance to heal, grow, and expand beyond the wildest dreams of an eight-year-old girl.

Even after spending a few years benefitting from

the group support of Alateen and Al-Anon, I still rejected the idea of "needing." I held on to the belief that I was the only person I could rely on. I avoided situations where I felt I owed anything to anyone, and that often meant not asking for help. This pattern of going it alone shifted with one phone call. At twenty-three years old, in a moment of desperation, sitting alone on the floor of my high-rise apartment overlooking the Denver skyline, I called a 24-hour crisis hotline for the Rape, Abuse & Incest National Network (RAINN). Though it had been many years since the most recent sexual assault, every day I lived with that fear, pain, and shame. Through my tears I asked for help, for comfort, for support.

My call to RAINN connected me to a local organization that worked with sexual assault survivors. I attended my first group for incest survivors, and later joined another group for rape and sexual assault survivors. I wasn't going through life alone anymore. The women in those support groups helped me more than they know.

I started seeking community in my personal life, too. In the late 90s, as internet communication was starting to become popular, I found community on a message board for Tori Amos fans where I made lifelong friends. I later joined Livejournal, an online social networking site before social networking was as popular as it is today. A group of friends I met on Livejournal to talk about *Buffy* and other TV shows, movies, and books we love has been meeting annually for over ten years. Through the internet, I was able to form lasting friendships over shared interests and shared life experiences. Though in many cases we lived in different states, even in different countries, making friends online was the first time in my life I felt I truly belonged.

In my thirties, I returned to the rooms of the Al-Anon Family Groups. I found education, friendship, and fun at Toastmasters International. Now, in my forties, I am part of a coworking community. I've been a part of various networking groups and associations over the years, including a group of emerging young professionals I've stayed connected with for over twenty years. Finally, in 2017, I took all I learned in those communities to start a local women's leadership organization in Northern Colorado, She Goes High.

She Goes High creates a fun, authentic, and welcoming space for women to give and receive support. It has grown into a thriving women's group, with events every month centered around the concerns of working women. While I understood such a group was an important piece missing from my life, I realized the significant impact the community has had on others when I received six separate nominations from She Goes High members and was recognized with a local women's business award. Finding a community is important for everyone!

I created She Goes High because I knew the value of peer support. Over the years, I surrounded myself with a support system that encouraged and motivated me as I created the better life I dreamed of when I was eight years old. Surrounding yourself with people who share similar interests and are working toward similar goals creates connections, encourages a sense of belonging, and provides friendship, experience, strength, and hope. Strong, supportive communities are one of the most important factors in personal and professional success—possibly in achieving success, and definitely in sustaining success.

> **Real growth, real transformation happens when you put this book down.**

If you're like me, you are comfortable and familiar being independent, relying on yourself, and doing it yourself. Maybe people have let you down. Or maybe you're afraid people won't like you, or it's easier to stay home. Relying on yourself may have gotten you this far, but this may be as far as it goes. To fulfill your potential, you need support. If you haven't already found your community, it's time to seek it out.

Self-help is limited. Real growth, real transformation happens when you put this book down. It happens when you find a group of amazing, inspirational people who, like you, know you are capable of more. It happens when you engage with these people and you lift each other up. It happens when you become something bigger than yourself alone.

I've got you covered. Join our community at **beautifulbadass.me**.

Too Big for Your Britches

As I write this book I often ask myself, who am I to be writing this book? I hear my grandmother's sharp, critical voice in my head and remember her bright red manicured nails digging into my arm leaving half-moon indentations in my skin. "Who do you think you are?" she sneers. "You're nobody special. You're no better than anyone else. You're getting too big for your britches."

I can stand on stage before an audience of hundreds and share the same stories and ideas I've written in this book and, sure, I feel nervous, yet telling my story live and in person is easier than writing it down as a bound, packaged, and finished product for you to read. I've done a lot of scary and brave things in my life and somehow writing this book is the scariest (so far) and requires the greatest amount of courage.

In childhood, I accepted the idea that I'm not special. Doing something as big and bold as writing a book is antithetical to that idea; it's arrogant and vain. Moreover, I fear that in writing this book I will be ostracized and rejected by my family and friends. Everyone who reads it will find out I'm a big failure! It will be in print—published for all the world to see and know the truth: Chrysta thinks she's better than us because she wrote a book, but she's really nothing more than an unlovable loser.

All of that is classic impostor syndrome.

Impostor syndrome is a psychological pattern in which an individual doubts their accomplishments and has a persistent internalized fear of being exposed as a "fraud." It wasn't a concept I related to immediately, but as I did more research on the topic, I found I experience impostor syndrome, too. Except, for me, I don't fear being exposed as a fraud so much as being exposed as a failure. I fear being exposed as the unworthy and pathetic girl I felt I was when I lived in poverty. That fear is the reason I waited so long to write this book. I'm done waiting. Here I am, writing. I hear those voices, those doubts, and I'm doing this anyway.

Too Big For Your Britches

A friend and business coach asked me, just a few months before I began writing this book, "Have you always been afraid of taking up your own space in the world?" Her question resonated with me—I had played small for much of my life. I wanted to shine, but never shine brighter than anyone else. I was happy to make my mark on the world as long as it didn't hurt, offend, or bother anyone. I avoided taking up my space—of fully showing up, of being seen and heard.

This book is me taking up my space in the world. I overcame all the rest of the shit in my life, so I can overcome my fear of writing a book, too. Based on what I've achieved, I know that writing a book must be possible, too. What is possible for you? What can you do that you or someone you love has told you that you can't do? What can you overcome? What risk are you willing to take by choosing the unknown future of your dreams over the unhappy, desperate reality you've been living in?

While I will offer unconditional pep, I can't tell you that you'll succeed because I succeeded. I don't know you. I don't know your circumstances. But are you so scared of failing that you're not willing to try? Take up your space in the world. Believe in yourself. Go ahead and be too big for your britches—you can buy new britches in the right size.

Redeemed

I wasn't popular in high school. I never quite felt like I fit in. Maybe everyone finds it difficult to relate in high school, but while other girls worried about who was going to ask them to prom and what grade they got on yesterday's math test, I worried about my mom's self injury, her next suicide attempt, and making sure the rent was paid so we weren't evicted again. On top of that I was a little too weird, a little too depressed, and definitely too poor.

I often couldn't afford to take part in social activities with my high school friends. Going to the movies was too expensive. If I tagged along with friends to eat out, I only drank water, stomach rumbling, while they enjoyed their meals. On a really good day, I was able to scrape together enough money for a soda or side of fries so I could join without making things awkward. If the city bus couldn't get me to the place my friends chose to meet, I needed a ride or I couldn't go. One of my high school friends once told me, "You can't do anything we want to do—it is hard to be friends with you."

That comment still hurts, and I choose to believe my high school friends were the best friends they knew how to be, doing their best to navigate life based on their own experience and perspective, just like I was. My life was unhappy and unstable, and maybe it was difficult for them to be friends with me.

Since leaving high school, I've had three opportunities to attend a high school reunion. Each one was a very different experience and a different snapshot of where I was on my journey.

I happily skipped my ten-year reunion. At the time, having recently separated from my first husband and on the brink of bankruptcy, I preferred to keep my failures to myself.

For my twenty-year reunion, I felt like I had something to prove. I wanted my classmates to know I made it. Surprise, I'm not a loser! I wanted to impress them, but the truth was only a handful of people noticed me at all. I saw a few old friends, had a nice enough time, but left feeling like I did in high school, a little insecure and self-conscious, feelings I now recognized that other people might have been feeling too.

I had a completely different experience at my twenty-five-year reunion. This time I had nothing to prove. I didn't care about impressing anyone. I showed up without an agenda. I showed up curious what the night would bring. I had no expectations. I was finally comfortable being seen as I am, not for what I had achieved or not achieved in my life. I was comfortable taking up my space in the world.

Showing up is a powerful experience. I allowed myself to be myself, authentically me, the perfectly imperfect person I am. At my twenty-five-year reunion I joyfully reconnected with a handful of old friends. I stood up and sang karaoke, belting out tunes unconcerned if I made a mistake and not caring what anyone thought of me. I was having fun and that's all that mattered to me. As I held the microphone, unironically and gleefully singing "Maybe This Time" from the musical *Cabaret*, I knew I was right where I wanted to be—being me. Being seen for me. Loving myself. Believing in myself.

I see the power in simply showing up and being your authentic self at every She Goes High meeting. She Goes High appreciates and celebrates every woman just as she is. It's not about having the right words, or about looking or acting a certain way. Every woman is welcome just as she is. This acknowledgment in the inherent brilliance and beauty in each of us, just as we are today, creates powerful connections in a community that helps women become better leaders and better versions of themselves. She Goes High has helped me be more comfortable showing up in all areas of my life.

As I edit this book I'm navigating yet another divorce. It has made the difficulties of writing even tougher as my home life is in flux and I now have several areas of my life feeling unsettled and unfamiliar. Through this transition I still show up every day in my business and my life. I show up whether I am experiencing hope and joy or grief and sadness. Being present and showing up helps me deal with the problems and take joy from the progress. Once again I am experiencing firsthand the power in showing up versus putting on a show.

I invite you to show up more fully in life. Show up in your strengths, your talents, and your vulnerability. Stop trying to be who you think you're supposed to be. Just be you. You're amazing, powerful, and beautiful just as you are. I see you. I celebrate you.

> **Stop trying to be who you think you're supposed to be. Just be you.**

Reality Check: Busting The Myth That Anything Is Possible

I started blogging in 2010 as blogs were just beginning to be a viable path to earn extra income or even replace a full-time income. When I started my blog, I felt frustrated by the overwhelming number of blogs promising anyone could quit their job and have a lucrative location-independent life through blogging. These blogs touted the advantages of entrepreneurship over traditional employment, painting those poor schmoes working 9–5 as dreary automatons destined to live unfilling, boring lives.

At the time, it was my dream to be an entrepreneur—who am I kidding, that's always been my dream—but I knew the promise of blogging for profit was not the right path for me. As much as I love writing, I didn't want to sell ads, write sponsored posts, or become an affiliate promoting someone else's products or services just to make money. I chose to write what I wanted to write, for me and me alone.

Despite not wanting to blog for profit, I bristled at the idea that earning a living through blogging was possible for everyone. My blog had a solid following, I attended blog conferences, I posted on social media, and I implemented most of the tricks to improve my blog's search engine optimization (SEO), but I lacked the stats to make money from blogging. Despite my best efforts and doing everything "right," my blog didn't gain the following for me to make it as a professional blogger.

> **Your actions and behaviors inform your success, but they do not guarantee it.**

As I read these other blogs promising freedom and financial success through blogging, I was confronted by an idea I had previously rejected: Anyone can have anything they desire if they just want it enough or if the right strategy is employed. Growing up with more than my share of hardships and setbacks, I've had plenty of life experiences that suggested all things are not equal. What I receive is not necessarily contingent on wanting or working hard enough. Your actions and behaviors inform your success, but they do not guarantee it. Whether or not you had a privileged upbringing, success isn't guaranteed. I've worked with plenty of career coaching clients who had opportunity, followed the expected path of college-marriage-career, only to find themselves stuck and struggling. You can do all the "right" things and still fail. Regardless of their level of privilege, my coaching clients who end up underemployed and underpaid have gone on to be successful and happy in their life and career. We worked together to find the way that works for them instead of following any particular formula for success.

Some people are better-suited for one path, and some people are better-suited for another path. Take entrepreneurship, for example. Some have the natural skills to be entrepreneurs, and others can learn them. And then there are some people who don't want that life, or don't have the tolerance for the instability of being an entrepreneur. I strongly oppose the idea that being an entrepreneur is ideal for everyone. It may or may not be for you. Creating a better life is all about finding what works for *you*. I've built a successful career and successful business following my own path by discovering what's true for me and building a life supported by my truth. Recognizing that I wasn't going to be a professional blogger supported me in finding the path that was right for me as a coach, speaker, and author.

You can't do everything you read about on the internet, but you can do *something*. What I mean is that you have to find your path and follow it, instead of trying to follow every path or follow the wrong path for

> Your life is your own, and your path will be unique to you.

you. If something in this book doesn't work for you, don't do it. Do the stuff that does work for you. Take what you like and leave the rest. Don't simply do what people expect of you. Don't try to become a professional blogger, or online entrepreneur, or CEO if it doesn't work for you. Screw what you "should" do. Do what you want. Find your way. Your life is your own, and your path will be unique to you. Don't listen to me or anyone else that tells you what's right for you. You decide what is right for you. Find your inner truth and trust it. Guard your truth fiercely. Protect it. Nurture it. There's always an opportunity to create something better for yourself, and your job is to find or create that for yourself. Are you ready to create?

It's Time to Tune In

It's time to tune in. It's time to receive.

Since I started receiving, I stopped protesting or feeling guilty when a friend offers to pick up the tab.

Since I started receiving, I started believing I'm worthy of the praise I'm given.

Since I started receiving, I stopped feeling like I have to keep score and give more, more, and then some more.

Since I started receiving, I don't question, analyze, or doubt opportunities and gifts that come my way.

When you receive, you allow other people to fill you up.

Let's say you invite all your friends over for a party. You set out color coordinated plates and napkins, a fancy cheese plate, and a bowl of refreshing raspberry punch. The cheese and punch are quickly consumed, and more guests are on the way. The doorbell rings and one friend arrives with a hummus and veggie tray, and the next friend contributes a bottle of wine. As

> **What if you received whatever good stuff someone had to give you and you received it openly and fully?**

additional guests arrive they bring more food and drink to share. In allowing others to contribute, your party is a huge success and everyone has a great time!

What could you accomplish if you not only practiced good self-care, but you took it a step further and allowed others to fill your cup? What if you received whatever good stuff someone had to give you and you received it openly and fully?

In the book *The Alchemist* by Paulo Coelho, the alchemist gives a monk a piece of gold worth far more than the debt he seeks to repay. The monk argues that the value of the gold goes beyond the value of the monk's generosity. The alchemist replies, "Don't say that again. Life might be listening, and give you less the next time." Are you protesting good things that come to you? How is that habit limiting what you're willing to receive?

It's easy to hold on to the bad stuff—when someone lets us down or puts us down. This we accept without question. And the good stuff—compliments and recognition and appreciation—these are the things we minimize, justify, or forget. If you want to do really amazing things, if you want to improve your situation, you need to get better at receiving. You need to be a hell of a lot needier! (Not in the whiny, I-can't-handle-my-shit way, but in the yes-I-need-help-sometimes-and-I'm-willing-to-receive-it way.)

I realize this idea might be the most challenging of all. At least it was the most challenging for me. I'm still learning how to receive, and how to accept and integrate the good stuff I receive. It's hard for me because for most of my life I believed that if I didn't work really, really hard for everything I had, that meant I was lazy, irresponsible, spoiled, or needy. Most of my life I couldn't let the good things in without knowing the reason I came by those good things—and it had to be a really good reason. I've realized how much this idea has limited what I am able to do because the really amazing things are going to take more resources, more gumption, and more sass than I've got on my own.

What are you open to receive? As this book comes to a close, I want to leave you with this invitation to receive. Receive this book. Receive each opportunity to improve your situation. Receive yourself as enough (you are enough).

Stop surviving and start thriving. Believe in you.

Acknowledgements

This is your book. Thank YOU for buying, reading, reviewing, and sharing it. Whether or not you enjoyed this book, even if you hated it, thank you for believing in yourself enough to read it. After all, this truly is your book. Take what you like and leave the rest.

This book is also mine. I wrote it with the love, support, encouragement, and guidance of many whom I will appreciate here.

Corey Bairre: You are silly. You are thoughtful. Thank you for years of shared laughter, patience, and love. I know wonderful and amazing things are in store for your future.

Mikki Burcher: You are a world-changer. You are a leader. Thank you for sharing your powerful insights and wisdom as a beta reader.

Sarah Davison-Tracy: You are empowering. You are inspiring. Thank you for witnessing my potential and encouraging me to take up my space in the world.

Deanna Estes: You are talented. You are knowledgeable. Thank you for guiding the look and design of this book with your many years of experience and your creativity.

Ariana Friedlander: You are wise. You are insightful. Thank you for leading the way as an author and badass.

John Garvey: You are hilarious. You are powerful. You are insightful. Thank you for many hours of writing sprints, discussions, walks, and laughter and friendship.

Carrie Lamanna: You are creative. You see into the heart of things. Thank you for listening to my rambling ideas and reflecting back what I shared with you in a thoughtful, coherent format. You are an amazing writing coach.

Nikki Larchar: You are inspired. You are hope. Thank you for the laughter and tears month after month over swirls at happy hour.

Candace Leczel: You are passionate. You are heartfelt. Thank you for your continued friendship, and thank you for your joyful support as a beta reader.

Alli Martin: You are a wordsmith. You are a badass editor. Thank you for helping my words have the greatest impact in the world, and thank you for being a dear friend.

Molly McCowan: You are a light. You are a leader. Thank you for starting and hosting Shut Up and Write Fort Collins, where much of this book was written (and revised and re-written and revised some more!)

Theresa Meyer: You are joyful. You are loving. Thank you for adding ease and inspiration to my Hawaii writing retreat.

Kerri Moncrief: You are sassy. You are kickass. Thank you for sharing your insight and wisdom as a beta reader.

Laura Morocco: You are wicked smart. You are a rock star. Thank you for sharing your heart and wisdom as a beta reader.

Acknowledgements

Jenny Morse: You are intelligent. You are fun. Thank you for happy hours, writing sprints, and giggling across the table at Shut Up and Write. Thank you for your insightful feedback as a beta reader. Thank you for your friendship.

Ellen O'Neill: You are an artist. You are intuitive. Thank you for bringing my words to life with your amazing illustrations.

Tami Parker: You are a leader. You are powerful. Thank you for your continued friendship, support, and encouragement, and thank you for the tiara!

Maureen Phillips: You are love. You are all heart. Thank you for being a cheerleader and supporter of me and my work. Thank you for your open and honest feedback as a beta reader.

Resources

This book is just the beginning. Your life gets better from here. Take what you've learned and practice it. Most change happens with the support and encouragement of community. Here's a few places you can find people working to change themselves and create a better life and a better world.

Beautiful Badass Community: Be a beautiful badass! Join us at **beautifulbadass.me**!

She Goes High Community: Practice taking up your space in the world. With multiple monthly events, retreats, conferences, masterminds, and more, She Goes High is here to encourage and celebrate you! Join us at **shegoeshigh.us**!

Alcoholics Anonymous (AA): AA is a fellowship available to anyone who is battling alcoholism and is seeking help to overcome it. Find a meeting in your area at **aa.org**.

Al-Anon Family Groups: Al-Anon members are people, just like you, who are worried about someone with a drinking problem. Find a meeting in your area at **al-anon.org**.

Art of Feminine Presence: Our world is in desperate need of feminine role models who are courageous enough to speak their truth and live the life they desire. Find a class or event near you at **theartoffemininepresence.com**.

National Alliance on Mental Illness (NAMI): NAMI is the nation's largest grassroots mental health organization dedicated to building better lives for the millions of Americans affected by mental illness. Get help at **nami.org**.

RAINN: RAINN is the nation's largest anti-sexual violence organization, providing support, education, and resources to survivors of sexual assault. It's never too late to get help at **RAINN.org**.

Toastmasters International: Toastmasters International can help you improve your communication and build leadership skills. Find a group in your area at **toastmasters.org**.

Vocabulary of Feeling Words

When you've lived your life in survival mode, you may have lost touch with the full range of your feelings. You may struggle to identify every emotion. Use this vocabulary of feeling words as a starting point.

Cynical	Frightened	Irritated
Delighted	Frozen	Isolated
Depleted	Frustrated	Joy
Depressed	Fulfilled	Jumpy
Determined	Furious	Knotted
Disappointed	Gentle	Lethargic
Disassociated	Gloomy	Light
Disconnected	Grateful	Listless
Discouraged	Grieving	Lively
Dissatisfied	Grouchy	Lonely
Distant	Grounded	Loose
Disturbed	Guilty	Loving
Doubtful	Happy	Lucky
Drained	Heartbroken	Melancholy
Dull	Heavy	Moody
Embarrassed	Helpless	Mortified
Empathy	Hesitant	Nervous
Empty	Hollow	Numb
Encouraged	Hopeful	Optimistic
Energized	Hopeless	Outraged
Engaged	Humbled	Overwhelmed
Enthusiastic	Humiliated	Painful
Excited	Impatient	Paralyzed
Exhausted	Incapable	Passionate
Expanded	Incompetent	Patient
Exposed	Indifferent	Peaceful
Fascinated	Inhibited	Perplexed
Flowing	Inspired/Inspiring	Playful
Fluid	Interested	Powerful
Forlorn	Intrigued	Powerless
Fragile	Irate	Present

Proud	Serene	Trusting
Questioning	Settled	Twitchy
Rattled	Shaken	Uneasy
Reflective	Shocked	Unhappy
Refreshed	Skeptical	Uninhibited
Regretful	Sorrow	Unsafe
Rejected	Sorry	Unsettled
Rejuvenated	Spacious	Unsure
Relaxed	Stiff	Untrusting
Reluctant	Still	Unworthy
Remorseful	Stimulated	Upset
Removed	Strong	Useless
Resentful	Suffocated	Vulnerable
Resigned	Suspicious	Weak
Resistant	Teary	Weary
Restless	Tender	Withdrawn
Rigid	Tense	Wobbly
Sad	Terrified	Wooden
Safe	Thankful	Worried
Satisfied	Thrilled	Worthless
Scared	Throbbing	Worthy
Self-conscious	Touched	
Sensitive	Trapped	

About the Author

Chrysta was put on anti-depressants when she was 8 years old after months of recurring nightmares, persistent depression, and suicidal ideation. She struggled with depression, anxiety, and post traumatic stress disorder throughout her childhood.

In high school her family lived in poverty. She couldn't afford to go out for french fries with friends, or to purchase a dress for performance choir. When she graduated high school she didn't receive her diploma due to less than $80 in unpaid school fees that her family could not pay.

That's when she realized she didn't have the same opportunities that other people had and that meant she had to create her own opportunities.

Over the next 20 years she created a successful professional career in human resources and accounting on her terms, without a college degree. She served on the Board of Directors for the Northern Colorado Human Resources Association and held multiple executive roles in Toastmasters International among other leadership roles in various non-profit and community organizations.

Through these experiences, she learned how business works. She learned what employers want. She learned to communicate with confidence. She shaped her own career path, leveraging on-the-job training. She found a way to work within a system that wasn't designed to work for her.

She had succeeded in business but was still struggling in life. At the age of 35, after years of health issues and a stress-induced bout of shingles, she realized she had more to learn. She started a work-life balance blog and discovered how to better manage stress, improve her health, and increase her happiness in work and life. People kept asking me how she did it. What was her secret? That's when she realized the next step was to help others find what she created for herself.

Chrysta founded her career coaching business, Live Love Work. She later founded and became the CEO of She Goes High, a women's leadership organization for introverts in Northern Colorado. After years of being asked, "when are you going to write a book," she started work on her first book, *Beautiful Badass: How To Believe In Yourself Against The Odds*.

Index

A

Al-Anon Family Groups 45, 192-193, 215
Anxiety. 10, 13-14, 20, 22, 27, 50, 85, 114, 169, 183-184
Art of Feminine Presence 185-187, 215-216
Attitude 2, 14-16

B

Bankruptcy 71-77, 100, 127, 200
Believing in yourself. 1, 11, 21, 25-30, 31-37, 43,
    46-48, 49-51, 53-55, 57-62, 66-67, 69, 71, 86, 106, 114, 119-120, 127,
    130, 138, 144-147, 151, 165-166, 184, 197, 209
Better life. . 3-4, 5, 7, 25-30, 42, 45-46, 53-54, 75, 82, 86, 99-101, 117, 120,
    124, 148, 154, 157, 159, 162, 191, 194, 205-206, 215-216
Boundaries. 33, 37, 42, 44, 97-101, 105-108, 109-112, 129, 166, 181

C

Choices. 11, 26, 34, 59, 77, 82, 88, 107, 123, 130, 154-156
Community 59, 177, 191-194, 201, 215
Comparing. 85-90
Confidence. 9, 34-35, 52, 61-62, 67, 86, 90, 92, 120, 123-126,
    130, 151, 178
Courage 5, 52, 57, 69, 76, 94, 111, 127, 130, 177, 191, 195
Create. 1-3, 13-14, 26, 29, 40, 44, 45-46,
    53, 80, 86, 109, 112, 117, 120, 124, 128, 131, 133, 154, 157, 159, 161,
    169, 182, 191, 193-194, 201, 206, 215

D

Depression. . . . 10, 13, 20, 22, 27, 29, 50, 55, 64, 66, 73, 85, 114, 163, 199
Desire. 11, 43, 157, 163-168,
Disappointing the right people 43, 79-83, 91, 110,
Divorce. 71-77, 100, 127, 153, 201

E

Expectations 10, 24, 49-50, 60, 86, 99, 102, 110, 128, 153, 156, 161, 166, 186, 201, 204, 206

F

Fear 11, 28, 33, 41, 50, 52, 60-61, 75, 108, 138, 156, 159, 192, 195-197

Forgiveness 22-24, 80

G

Gratitude 13-20, 40, 121, 125-126, 140, 146, 149-151

H

Happiness 13-14, 17, 22, 27, 33, 46, 51, 71, 73, 88, 91, 93, 99-100, 128, 133-134, 154-155, 163, 168, 172, 179, 197, 200, 205

Hope 5, 8, 13-14, 18, 26-27, 46, 66-67, 80, 194, 202

I

Impostor syndrome 50-51, 165, 196

Interpersonal abuse & violence 3, 13, 25, 72-73, 108, 109, 112, 136, 192

Intuition 10, 43, 169-173, 213

J

Joy 14-18, 30, 40, 44, 55, 89-90, 91, 120, 141, 164, 169, 179-181, 187, 201-202

N

Negativity 14, 16, 37, 47, 87, 90, 102, 154-155, 172, 177, 180, 208

P

People-pleasing 31, 58-59, 79-82, 91, 93, 96, 106

Perfectionism 21-22, 29, 36, 43, 54, 87, 119-122, 179-182, 201

Positivity 1, 14, 16, 18, 47, 60, 87, 103, 108, 151, 154-155, 169, 172, 180, 182

Poverty............1-3, 10, 13, 25, 27, 50, 76-77, 85, 108, 112-113, 116,
     127, 135-137, 153, 163, 196, 199
Privilege..............................1-2, 85, 141, 159, 177, 204-205

R
Receiving..... 33, 43, 135-138, 139-141, 143-148, 149-151, 204, 207-209
Relationships..................32-37, 60, 71-75, 80, 97-100, 112, 166

S
Saying no....................... 37, 42, 91-96, 105, 109, 129, 157
Safety ... 2, 10, 13-15, 18, 98, 107, 109, 136, 153, 157, 165, 169, 171, 180
Self-care.................. 13, 39-44, 54, 100-101, 107-108, 121, 208
Self-doubt..................... 11, 49-52, 53, 123, 159, 161, 196, 207
Self-kindness.. 21-24, 55
Self-love................................45-48, 54, 76-77, 121, 126
Self-trust........... 10, 29, 37, 49-50, 52, 58-59, 92, 169-173, 183, 206
She Goes High.............................. 35, 193-194, 201, 215
Success...2, 8, 10-11,
     13, 34-36, 47, 50-51, 61-62, 74, 76, 80, 85-90, 105-108, 117, 123, 128,
     133, 143, 145, 147, 172, 177, 180-181, 191, 194, 204-205, 208
Suicide................................25, 27, 64, 66, 115, 199
Support............ 1, 10, 22, 27, 32, 39, 41-42, 44, 45-46, 59-60, 77, 96,
     107, 109, 117, 130, 133, 147, 155, 173, 175, 177, 185, 191-194, 205
Survivor and Survivorship.............3, 12, 13, 16, 29, 40-42, 54, 62,
     108, 153-155, 163-164, 169, 180, 192, 209, 216

T
Therapy 27, 39, 45, 75, 154-155
Thriving 3, 42, 108, 110, 193, 209
Trauma.............................. 1-2, 127, 136, 153-154, 180

Y
Yoga 120-121, 184-185, 187, 197-188

www.ingramcontent.com/pod-product-compliance
Lightning Source LLC
Chambersburg PA
CBHW031106080526
44587CB00011B/842